INNER EYE, LISTENING EAR

By the same author
SURVIVAL OF DEATH
LIVING ON
HIDDEN MAN

Editor of
THE BARBANELL REPORT

INNER EYE, LISTENING EAR

An Exploration Into Mediumship

PAUL BEARD

*Ah! Psyche, from the regions which
Are holy land*
    Edgar Allan Poe

PILGRIM BOOKS   BOOKS
TASBURGH   NORWICH   ENGLAND

Copyright © Paul Beard 1992

All rights reserved. No part of this
publication may be reproduced, stored
in a retrieval system, transmitted in
any form or by any means electronic,
mechanical, recording or photocopying,
or otherwise, without prior permission
from the publishers.

British Library Cataloguing-in-Publication Data

A catalogue record of this book
is available from The British Library
ISBN 0 946259 41 0

Photoset by Waveney Typesetters, Norwich
and printed in Great Britain at the University Press, Cambridge

Dedicated to

The early pioneers whose courage
achieved so much

CONTENTS

Chapter		Page
	Preface	ix
1	Mediumship: A Preview	1
2	The First Approaches To A Session	14
3	The Medium At Work: Early Levels	21
4	The Recipient's Task and Responsibility	43
5	Psychical Research and Mediumship	63
6	The Communicator	81
7	The Medium At Work: Inner Levels	93
8	Self-mediumship	106
9	The Mentor	117

PREFACE

A few sections of this book, in somewhat altered form, have been used in lecturing at the College of Psychic Studies and at the Society for Psychical Research, and other parts have appeared in the C.P.S. journal *Light*. In reclaiming this material for reproduction and realignment, I would like to thank those bodies for their courtesy.

In the interests of clarity I have largely referred to mediums as feminine, and to communicators and recipients as masculine. All three, of course, can equally be of the opposite gender.

I would especially emphasise that there are many excellent male mediums.

Paul Beard

CHAPTER ONE

MEDIUMSHIP: A PREVIEW

1

MEDIUMSHIP IS BOTH a simple and a complex happening. To evaluate what is involved, an important balance needs to be sought between objective and subjective sides. Both must necessarily contribute if a long term and developing view is to come about. Since mediumistic material also arises at very different levels of significance, this requires to be assessed by criteria appropriate to each level.

The immediate and obvious purpose of mediumship lies of course in whether it provides evidence of survival of death or whether all that is said can be explained away as derived from earth sources. Evidence having been given, other deeper factors come to be sought. A serious approach is called upon to recognise the levels involved. It is easy to become too credulous or too dismissive. It is misleading and sometimes malicious to judge all by its most superficial levels. These are often the ones first met with and provide material for the usual caricature image of a medium as a corpulent elderly lady functioning behind a bead curtain, and (in more than one sense) in the dark. It could equally well be an image of a highly sensitive and refined being like 'Mrs. Willett' working privately with and for high grade psychical researchers and classical scholars, and for no financial reward. Mediumistic material can be trivial, vague and incomplete. On the other hand it can work in areas of deep perception.

Extrasensory perception, the basis of mediumship, is a little-understood faculty. There can be no one answer as to what mediumship is. Its expression is according to the depth of attunement each medium finds it possible to reach, and also according to the depth and sincerity of response each recipient can find in himself. The recipient both contributes indirectly to the situation and often also limits it, consciously or unconsciously.

What then makes a medium different from other human beings? In most ways not very much. What is really important is the true source of her material, and how clear its meaning and value. Mediumship does not exist in a void. If these gifts are real ones it is most unlikely that they would not function at times to a lesser degree in non-mediumistic persons also, and appear spontaneously in other than the usual mediumistic forms. There is a great deal of evidence that they do so, anecdotal since it arises spontaneously. It resembles, but is wider than, the sensitivity often demonstrated in civilised and intimate social relationships where it is on the verge of, and occasionally passes into, telepathy. Good hostesses use telepathy, or near telepathy, and often well perceive what is in their guests' thoughts and feelings, but telepathy can also extend well beyond a hostess's direct or oblique deductions.

Other extrasensory experience which can arise in non-mediums, usually comes unexpectedly – perhaps only once in a lifetime. Often it is at a crisis situation, material or spiritual, which brings about a momentarily raised sensibility, and at times strongly suggests, as well, a discarnate presence.

Telepathy, however, is by no means limited to heightened areas of sensibility. As is well known telepathy operates frequently in tribal life, perhaps because there the mind is not cluttered with the many encumbrances of education in civilised beings. In primitive peoples an easier route seems able to open up. The silence of the bush, like many other types of silence, is favourable for the inner listening where telepathy operates clearly. Telepathy is largely accepted in tribal life as a method of distant communication, and often also what is taken as communication with ancestors.

Mediums use telepathy in a more regular and orderly way. For ordinary persons telepathy largely operates in their own personal and private context. Mediums are able to go further than this, to use it in a third party way on behalf of others. What they perceive is not their business but that of their clients.

In the civilised world a professional medium is obliged to make daily use of her specialised sensitivity for the benefit of people's life situations. Problems, real or illusory, are brought to her. She needs access then to deeper vision than her listeners have been able to reach for themselves, and than her own when speaking as a private person. Sometimes an overwhelming impression arises of another mind at work of quite different calibre from the medium's own. It is not surprising that at other times her message can occasionally be cloudy and clumsy. When the originating message is transmitted, its ideas and feelings can then suffer a mis-direction during imperfect mediumistic processes both of listening and then of interpreting.

Obviously mediumship cannot be well judged until some of its working difficulties are recognised. Sifting the material requires a very conscientious approach. Sometimes, if the message is to be correctly understood an element of partnership becomes necessary, requiring a considerable deal of integrity to overcome difficulties of interpretation. What is the communicator really trying to say? Through human imperfection clues which arise can go astray.

Mediumship is perhaps best looked upon in an overall way as a specialised branch of a general sensibility which all of us have in however slight a degree, much as all have a rudimentary talent for some form of art but in most not large enough to be useful and sometimes so slight as to be hardly perceptible. It is also a talent somewhat resembling that of an interpretive artist in that it is both natural and trained. Training is partly by discarnate helpers, partly by another medium, but more importantly by self-training. It needs to be combined with dedication and constant self-discipline. Also, like the work of an interpretive artist, mediumship does best when given a worthwhile and honest response. At times when mediums are partially dependent on their clients' skills for accurate perception of the intended meaning, mistakes readily arise. The client thus contributes both for good and ill, especially when there needs to be a partnership of discovery.

Some mediums possess a slightly unusual physical make-up, just as do some outstanding artists and athletes – Nijinsky's foot, Bannister's lungs, a singer's depth of breath. Most mediums require a ready ability for dissociation. As one medium said with a twinkle, 'I am a loose woman'. She meant that whilst working she needed to be able to stand outside her own normal thought and feeling patterns, freeing herself to be open to that of others she takes to be discarnate persons.

Another useful comparison can be made between mediumship and art in terms of the road to achievement. For every five fine artists, and every fifty good ones, there are five thousand feeble amateurs or non-achievers due to failures in skill, in training, in dedication. It is essential also to recognise that a medium encounters communicators of very varying skills and character. A communicator can only describe what he finds as far as his own stature can take him. As Maurice Barbanell, a life-long medium, said after his death, 'I am learning . . . that knowledge, like liquid, can only be contained in a receptacle that has equal capacity'. In other words his stature limits his cognition. Mediumship reflects the same rule. A humdrum medium can be accurate in her way but she often only reaches part of the story. Her picture of her communicator's nature and interests will fall short and be described only in her own humdrum terms. If she paints a picture of how life is lived hereafter this will be humdrum too. What marks out the high quality medium is a precision, a razor sharpness, a hitting of the mark and, especially, the defining or distinguishing of emotional situations exactly.

Thus mediums differ very considerably in their accuracy and depth of perception. This is dictated by their inner spiritual quality more than by their technical skills. When, in the interests of psychical research, it is sought to eliminate the subjective field, this invariably impoverishes the material. In medical and transpersonal psychology, on the contrary, much has come to be accepted which is full of subjective material but where in time general modes of behaviour can clearly be observed at work. In the extrasensory field subjective material calls for detached yet intuitive and sensitive interpretation. At times too some mediumistic insights touch closely upon fields known in inner religious experiences.

Mankind enjoys attempting to divide and conquer experience by creating separate orderly fields of study. Life, however, has a habit of expanding experience from one field into different areas and insists upon presenting a seemingly untidy whole. In addition to its unfamiliarity, mediumistic communication partakes of something of this multiple character as it shifts from one level to another, making it elusive and hard to judge. Communicators, obviously, do not all feel and think alike and it would be a gross over-simplification to suppose that all encounter exactly the same experiences after death, or evaluate them similarly.

2

After the early evidence provided, the worthy recipient can expect that a more active linking up with former earth companions can be looked for. These may have some advice to give. We make our own judgments on what they say. It is necessary, when comparatively recent arrivals describe the life around them, to be cautious since seasoned communicators warn us that such accounts have more misunderstanding in them than is yet known by those who tell them. So one must be ready for limitations and unintended error. The pictures given will differ since each sees only according to his own ability.

Further on than this level true spiritual teachers appear. They are of various grades. In parenthesis there can also be false or mischievous beings posing as teachers. True teachers will be found to be little concerned with personality issues. These are *our* prison bars. They suggest we can leave our prison as soon as we wish. That is not easy because it also involves of course leaving behind some of the qualities of character which have put us in prison in the first place. These teachers speak simply. Their teachings are easier to understand than to apply. They do not wish us to become personally attached to them though their goodwill is very evident. Without doubt one gradually comes to feel a sense of superior stature, and that they are likely to know more than they choose as yet to impart. Whilst engaged in our earth purposes we are unlikely to be in touch with more than a part of their total being. To reach us they tell us that they are obliged in some way to condense and limit themselves as well as their message in order to come closer to our level.

This book does not deal with how to learn to become a medium. This is best left to the professionals. It concerns itself as best it can with three levels of mediumship, in turn each requiring a separate standpoint, since truth has many facets calling in turn for the degree of understanding appropriate to each. First is the level of personal evidence and reassurance. Next local advice and a preliminary but limited and varying account of what has happened soon after death.

And third, the field of spiritual insight from senior beings, offering changes and challenges in how we conduct our life. At each level the field of observation alters. What makes sense at one level does not necessarily appear to do so when seen from lower levels, nor from higher levels than its own.

It is not difficult to make a picture of mediumship as possessing, as do so many activities, a number of levels of excellence or the reverse. The medium usually works, though not necessarily always, at a level of consciousness where she finds herself at ease. Other occasions arise when she is overtaken by an accumulation of material which she little understands, but feels strongly impelled to impart. At such times there will be more of the communicator inherent in the material and less of the medium. At important moments it is as if her consciousness is raised for a moment; something beyond her habitual levels finds its way to her.

An important part of the purpose of this book is to show that the medium is able to work upon an interior ladder of which several steps are available to her. Mediumship is certainly not to be understood without a recognition of this. It can also be seen, however, that the ladder of the medium is not the only one involved. The whole field is flexible enough for communicator and recipient as well as the medium each to have their own ladder. The higher the step on which each is able to stand, the deeper the meaningfulness which can be imparted and received.

Therefore, whilst the responsibility falls mostly upon the medium, communicator and recipient alike contribute from where they stand upon their own ladder. Each of the three can at times let the other two down. Without doubt, all need to contribute with the fullness of their integrity, else the result suffers. The more each of them is able to listen and receive in the right way, the better the result. All three have essential roles.

It will come to be seen that each contributes or fails to do so, and maximum harmony between all three will lead to the best results, and perhaps even enable the medium temporarily to work on a step she has never reached before.

There is thus a much greater intricacy in the whole interwoven purpose than at first is likely to be recognised.

So evidence of survival to establish identity is the basic step, however important at first. As one medium put it, it is only the postman's knock. Mediumship can pass on at later stages to the deeper parts of human make-up, our inner kingdom lost or not yet found, or only slightly sensed, and reflect other parts of the inner world which range beyond the early, close at hand, shores on which we first land after death.

3

The next section of communication, in part overlapping the first, concerns the nature of experience in the next world. It is important always to bear in mind that information is in line with the communicator's ability to recognise and absorb what is around. Where have they changed, where are they the same? What experiences have they had since they died? And what effect has this had upon their character and outlook? Are they still very recognisable? This brings its own kind of conviction, like that of listening to a good witness. A good witness usually comes over as also having a character of worth.

In other cases information is suspect when it appears to picture something remarkably like this world but without its drawbacks. Max Heindel names this early area the 'desire world'. These accounts often describe the beauties and the harmonies in the inner world. It is necessary to be careful here. These advertised facilities contain different aspects within them. One aspect is the very simple one of finding freedom from the burdens of being encased in a physical body with its discomforts and disobediences in old age. As a close friend said: 'I found myself feeling so very well that this made me realise I must have passed over'. Such a feeling is not due to our merit, it is part of the structure of existence, much as sleep brings refreshment to all. Another aspect has been pointed out for many years, and perhaps increasingly so more recently, – the heaven which Spiritualistic doctrine promises so readily, usually known as the Summerland, is partly made up of elements of our own creation. This is why it is called a desire world. Much of it is what we want heaven to be, containing those things of which earth life has deprived us. It is something of a domesticated heaven. Here we are, so to speak, with our loved ones and friends in a comfortable railway carriage which has a beautiful view through the window, and on our way to a permanent holiday. Sometimes it takes quite a time to realise that the carriages have no engine attached to them. In the better phrase of that intense and passionate spirit Frederic Myers, speaking some thirty years after his death, the Summerland is illusion where 'the soul can adapt the memory world to his taste', projecting the emotional life and desires of his earth existence, 'but he dreams back in order that he may be able to go forward once more on his journey'. Thus illusion in the early areas of the inner world is not wasted. Like earth illusion we can learn from it. However it does not appear to be easy for all to leave the train and begin to walk for themselves. Nor will any be forced to; each must choose for himself.

4

Having basked in the sun for a while, as a teacher has put it, one then becomes aware that a cloud is gradually creeping up. In this cloud one begins to be shown often disguised faults and incompletenesses which one has carried around as part of one's character, which are still there, and will still be there until we choose to do something to remove them. It is then that the pilgrim in the inner world finds that after all there is a great deal of hard work to be done, and much of the hard work is upon his own character. He has to face, in short, a degree of spiritual reality at a deeper level than he managed to acknowledge when upon earth.

To give an example of what will seem to be of the stuff of true communication at an early level, there was an intellectual who had a considerable knowledge of psychic matters. Unfortunately he gradually came to feel that in his marriage he had rather outgrown his wife. One part of himself almost came to despise a part of her. He died a few years before his wife and when she rejoined him he found that he was not the more spiritually advanced one as he had thought, but that she was. She was the one who had made the sacrifices in the marriage. Being an honest man he returned and gave this information. In the inner world things are not concealed as they often are on earth.

So in time all discover what they really are, and it is likely to provide a certain amount of surprise, by no means always of a pleasant kind. It becomes quite clear that, just as on earth, worthwhile spiritual knowledge and increased spiritual depth have to be earned as well as learned. They are far from being a gratuitous gift which comes about just from the privilege of dying.

Much help is therefore given, and this is where the learning comes in. Learning is available at every level but it appears that important learning can come about which is of a different kind from the book learning we know on earth. It is nearer to reaching a realisation which comes from within and brings its own conviction with it. In order to make proper subsequent use of it, it calls in turn for the growth of new qualities. What is taught through serious mediumistic reception offers deeper meanings than is usually expected before coming into contact with it, and in order to find this it is a necessary task to try and disentangle the superficialities and illusions which many tolerate on earth and sometimes accept for the sake of ease. Instead, each is required gradually to find the essential core of his being, and to take hold of new values which come into his perception.

When a medium reaches inwardly for material, the recipient gradually learns and comes to accept that what is communicated, as Barbanell said, necessarily has to take the shape of the containing vessel. This includes that of the communicator as well as that of the medium, and that of the recipient himself. Thus it is most important, indeed essential, to recognise that all communication of a mediumistic kind is really a partnership made up of three persons, the medium, the communicator and the recipient, and spiritual limitations in each will disturb the quality of the whole.

The next world then cannot be seen fully objectively, either by those in it, or by ourselves, for man himself limits it. It is obvious that accounts must differ, according to whether the speaker is, say, a Mozart or a Hottentot. One would hardly expect the same story from each. So in seeking to discover something of the nature of the next world it is better to think of it as the coming about of a gradual awareness of a wider consciousness which permeates all that is around one, and also can be found playing upon ourselves. By working upon one's character, by altering it, one gradually then becomes aware of these deeper values. In other words one deepens one's vessel so that it is enabled to encompass more, and to participate gradually, little by little, in those parts of life which are at present beyond it.

In endeavouring to come to know a little more of ethical and spiritual matters in the next world, the early stages here are likely to be from accounts from persons who have been there for some while and can look backward and forward to some degree. This can be valuable but not so valuable as from one best described as a spiritual elder, whose range we come to recognise is a good deal wider still.

Some recipients, of course, are hard-headed, and why should they not be so? Others, more readily receptive, gradually find themselves coming into tune with meanings behind the outer sense of the teacher's words. They are learning something of the true processes of assimilation. The man of hard-headed values is neither more nor less important than the more receptive person. He is fulfilling at present a different function in the acquisition of knowledge, and throws out what he can neither use nor see any sense in. When dealing with communications and communicators it is necessary to be a little wary in not making up one's mind too soon about what the communicator is really saying or hinting. As said earlier the communication process is hampering him, and according to his stature the listener can be hampering it also.

When a later artist makes a copy of a great painting something is always lacking. He is not able to match the original, since the eye and the sensibility which make the copy are inferior to those of the primary artist. But it points towards it. It is merely the best picture one artist can yet paint in the early days of his journey. In one sense the first-met shores after death too are themselves an imperfect copy of what will be reached later.

5

It can be said that deeper teachers take an over-look into us. One often feels they are well aware, not only of our past, but also of the future which is due to unfold, already latent within us, but as yet unfulfilled. Hence they can sometimes see ahead the spiritual problems and conflicts inevitably awaiting us.

It is clear from accounts at many different levels that love, both personal and impersonal, is present in a way not often recognised on earth, and that it forms part of the very texture of the inner world. It imparts itself, somewhat as the sun imparts its rays universally. This is part of the realisation already mentioned.

The deeper teachers are little concerned with earthly institutions and dogmas, they are concerned with helping us one by one to tune ourselves up, to increase our capabilities of character, to defeat our own self-created devils, to be more at peace with ourselves and others. We can use this in our individual problems on earth. Hence their patience with us.

The pupil comes to recognise a call to inner or outer action and if he chooses to be obedient, he will discover a gradual change is coming about in him or herself. This is their way of teaching. These are subtle things, and of course they have a pastoral aspect. An important thing is that the pupil is always left to his own free will. It is by the use of it that in time he voluntarily casts off his limitations. Freedom does not lie at all in doing what one wants, it lies in learning to escape from the bondage of ourselves. Eventually, however far ahead, we can each pay the price required to become at last a free spirit.

In the following chapters we will look a little more closely at these basic facets of experience and endeavour to see what they are leading us to find and to become.

CHAPTER TWO

THE FIRST APPROACHES TO A SESSION

A LARGE NUMBER of mediumistic sessions are unavoidably spoiled or diminished because the listener is unfamiliar with the process, and with what is appropriate to his role. Since a correct response is important, even in early approaches, let us look at the *ABC* of the matter and consider how the recipient can best help rather than hinder.

The sitting is by appointment. Communicators may have made careful preparation for it. What the machinery is that allows them to know of this appointment beforehand is not fully understood, it is likely that some form of telepathic resonance operates. Of course the medium usually does not know who the sitter is to be. To provide the correct conditions for a complicated thing like communication through a third party in the person of a medium, it does not seem unlikely that, as in television, technicians work behind the scenes. If this is so, it is, to say the least, disappointing both to the intending communicators and to a supporting team if at the last moment the sitter cancels, deciding the office or the hairdresser is more important.

The medium too will have prepared for the sitting by reaching a certain quiescence, a still pool, a highly sensitised and vulnerable condition, to enable her to mirror what the communicator wishes to tell. A sitter who arrives agitated, late, or in an atmosphere of hurry and bustle, is likely to

THE FIRST APPROACHES TO A SESSION

disturb this pool. 'I just popped in to buy one or two things on the way. I couldn't find the place. I thought I would never get here. Now where did I put my notebook?'. It is necessary to leave the sitting in the hands of the medium; and to try to enter the room with a quiet mind, and so reflect something of the same condition as the sensitive needs for herself. It is best to be present at least ten minutes before the interview, in order to compose the mind. Unpunctuality also imposes a nervous strain upon the sensitive who will be tuned in to her specialised level of attention in order to be ready, and delay can adversely affect her.

If these factors are accepted, the enquirer will be better prepared. At the first interview all recipients are likely to be in a state of some emotional or nervous tension, and this is natural enough. It is partly due to the unfamiliarity of the process, and partly due to feelings, sometimes very intense ones, on facing the possibility of communicating with someone dearly loved, and perhaps thought to have disappeared for ever. Though a recipient cannot be expected to overcome this tension altogether, he will do best to try to allow it to subside. It will help the sensitive and therefore the success of the interview if he can manage a degree of control over his feelings.

Having said this, it remains wiser not to expect immediate contact with someone very close; though it is not an invariable rule, it is better to allow some weeks, or even months, after death to elapse. The one he is seeking can well need to adjust and to understand something of his new condition before he feels ready to attempt to communicate. Therefore it does not do to be disappointed if the contact first made is not with the person hoped for, who may need to be given more time.

It is highly preferable, if possible, to make a tape recorded account of what is said, which of course includes also the remarks made by the recipient. Even experienced persons find their memory has afterwards unconsciously coloured

INNER EYE, LISTENING EAR

some of the information and given it a different slant. Most sensitives, though not all, accept the use of a tape recorder, but if the sensitive objects then recourse will have to be made to shorthand or longhand notes. However, only with a complete record will it be possible later on to assess the evidence fully and accurately.

If the sensitive asks whether information she gives is correct, it is suggested that the recipient confines himself as far as possible briefly to affirming or denying in an honest way. Sensitives need to feel they are on the right wavelength and that the communicator with whom they are in touch is known to the sitter. When replying, special care should be taken not to give away evidence by adding extra facts. It is for the sensitive to try to provide these, and she will feel frustrated if her listener provides them first. The interview will be twice as convincing too if the communicator is left to produce them. The sitter should not stonewall, become impatient, or assume an inwardly suspicious or cynical attitude. The sensitive will quickly sense this. Investigators sometimes set traps in order to confuse the sensitive or put her off the track. This is unwise, for sensitives, whilst working, are in a highly suggestible state, and will sometimes respond, without being fully aware of it, to the investigator's false suggestions. When this happens it is largely the investigator who brings about errors for which he will then blame the sensitive. Fully accurate mediumship is difficult and it is much better to 'play fair' in order to allow the sensitive to produce as much positive information as possible, for it is by this that the material must primarily be judged. It is most important therefore to allow the sensitive to take the lead. It is both sensible and fair for her to be allowed full opportunity to work as well as possible *in her own way*. Analysis needs to be done afterwards and certainly not during the interview.

If the sitter is given the opportunity to listen to advice, his task is to accept it impartially and be very careful not to try to influence the sensitive into saying what he would most like to hear about his intended or possible future actions, or concerning emotional factors in his life. If he does intrude it is probable that he will unwittingly colour the mind of the medium. Advice received under these circumstances is unlikely to represent correctly what the communicator wishes to say, and confusion will result. Above all, care is essential not to distort what is conveyed in order to make it better fit the facts. Strict honesty is called for, and not all listeners discipline themselves to give it.

Experience shows that the communicator's difficulties too can be very considerable, for he too can be a tyro who has plenty still to learn abut communicating. Not to allow for this can bring about considerable misjudgment on the sitter's part, and subsequent disappointment and criticism. Beginners tend to assert that a known communicator 'would not have said that'. But supposing the communicator has changed, or supposing the medium paraphrases? It is also easy for the inexperienced recipient to suppose that the person he knew possesses, during the moments of communication, a completely ready grasp of all details of former earth memory. This is not so, and forms a complex problem. The evidence suggests that in order to communicate, it is often necessary to concentrate wholly upon the memory of a certain part of one's past life on earth, and in doing so temporarily to lose touch with other parts. For this reason it is necessary for the client to avoid abrupt changes of subject. It is a very natural mistake to assume that the communicator has only to speak the all-important proof needed, and for the medium then to relay it. Unfortunately things are far from being so easy, even in passing on everyday things like pet-names or surnames. The medium sometimes has to pick up a telepathic impression of a name without any prior knowledge of it, and this is often best done by a picture. Rose, as a Christian name, is easy because the medium can readily recognise a picture of such a well-known object. But how would a telepathic impression of a surname be conveyed if it were, say, Braithwaite or Donnelly? It is easy to conclude that the person so much hoped for cannot be present since he or she sometimes apparently seems ignorant of outstanding events and obvious facts in the former earth life, but the communicator may be helpless to bridge a gap to impress upon the medium's mind what he so much wants to say. He cannot but accept the medium's own difficulties or failures. At times the communicator has to try to get the message across by going a long way round, or may have to wait for a later occasion or for a different sensitive. It is rewarding to be patient, and not to become disappointed too soon.

Communicators are obviously limited to such part of the medium's mind as they are able to reach, and this mind is of course no mechanical instrument, but a living thing, with its own susceptibilities, responses and prejudices which sometimes adds its own comments and colourings; this must be watched for. Communicators too are at first not much wiser than they were on earth, though their present perspective may be a slightly wider one. They are certainly not a near-infallible source of information, as unfortunately is sometimes assumed on any subject the recipient's whim chooses to bring up. What is spoken must always be put before the court of the listener's own judgment before accepting it. The listener needs to be ready at times to stretch his own mind to reach correctly the intended meaning, as does often come about too in everyday earth situations.

When communication is flowing freely, and there is harmony between communicator, sensitive and recipient, excellent evidence and comment can be given and the recipient, in spite of working difficulties, can receive a very lively impression of the communicator's continuing knowledge of and loving interest in him or her. This is the real stuff of early communication.

THE FIRST APPROACHES TO A SESSION

Every enquirer, however, becomes concerned at some time lest all the material really only resides in his own mind and is drawn thence telepathically by the sensitive. It is useful to ask from whose viewpoint the material is given – from the enquirer's own viewpoint or from that of the communicator? Much more than facts are concerned. What is pictured may represent a very different temperamental attitude from the listener's own. He also needs to judge whether what is said throws new light upon his own situation, is helpful and loving, and is different from his own viewpoint. If these factors are strongly present, something other than telepathy drawn from his own mind can reasonably be considered likely.

Communicators often say that they are surprised to find not how little, but how much they are able to get through, in view of the difficulties they discover in the process, including being overridden by the medium. Even those who when on earth had knowledge and experience of the subject almost invariably state that they find that communication is far harder than they had expected. It requires concentration of considerable depth, hard for some communicators to find, and harder still to sustain.

Trance interviews are not often given to inexperienced clients. The sensitive, in going into trance, lays herself open to certain dangers, and thus needs first to come to feel confidence in the client's integrity. When the first trance interview does come about, it is essential to recognise that at the moments of going into, and also of emergence from trance, the sensitive is highly vulnerable to the slightest noise, which in her dissociated state can be almost unbearably painful and can create considerable nervous stress. It is like being without an outer skin. Therefore the sitter should be sure to remain completely quiet at these moments.

In trance the communicator is less likely to be a friend or a relative, but someone experienced and well used to the particular sensitive, whose task is to relay messages from those who would still find it too difficult to communicate directly. Nor, if a relative or friend appears on later occasions, should one expect to hear the familiar voice known on earth; the apparatus used will be the medium's own vocal equipment.

Eventually contact may be made with an entirely different level of communicator, with one who claims to be the sitter's particular mentor or teacher. This is an important moment, and it heralds a very significant relationship. No undue authority however must be given to any teacher simply because he is speaking from beyond death. If genuine he will disclaim such authority and ask his pupil to use his own judgment. This is a reassuring feature in communication. It is wise to respect it and do one's part accordingly. Such a teacher does not come to give material help, or to make for the pupil what should be his own decisions. His purpose is a spiritual one, in order gradually to help and encourage inner growth, which can only come about by the pupil's own efforts. The teacher can point to the path but the listener has to decide whether to try and walk it.

CHAPTER THREE

THE MEDIUM AT WORK: EARLY LEVELS

1

IT SOON BECOMES clear then that mediumship is able to function upon a number of different levels, and its character changes or deepens accordingly. It is very important to bear this always in mind. Whatever its level, the first task of the medium is to be truthful to that level. It will necessarily take place in an everyday context when one or more of the triangle concerned – communicator, medium, listener – cannot reach deeper. At another time the same medium can be in touch with a communicator who is speaking at a considerably deeper level. It is not the medium's fault if listeners block her efforts by coming with a selective filter, or who offer a variety of unhelpful obstacles.

It is incorrect to suppose a communicator is necessarily telling all he has come to say, much less all he knows; sometimes he has to limit himself, though he may be possessed of much material which he could utilise through a different sensitive or to a different recipient. The medium can be limited in the same way as a recipient by her shallowness of attention and poverty of sensibility and vocabulary. Sometimes too the communicator cannot overcome difficulties in retaining a link with the medium; he is defeated by the process itself. A deeper degree of concentration than he can manage is called for.

INNER EYE, LISTENING EAR

So the field of mediumship available can be hindered by psychological blocks arising in any of those concerned with its production. The processes of communication can become familiar but the true limitations of consciousness can remain. Early levels of mediumship are often in terms of a simple conveying of thoughts, feelings and memories of the recent earth life. Perhaps in time the communicator is able to tell a little of where he now finds himself, and of the natural and moral laws he sees as governing his new life. The recipient is able in time, if he retains his humility, to form some judgment of how deeply his communicator can reach in terms of such experience, and in understanding of that experience. Is he entitled, so to speak, to claim to be a lance-corporal or corporal in the ranks of communicators but hardly beyond that? What then of the generals and colonels? Such a rank will not be external of course; it becomes recognised by its deeper understanding, a wider and more true love, and a fuller power of participation in the life around him or her.

True mediumship is a difficult and skilled profession. Even the simplest practitioner, for instance, has to discover for herself where to place her material, to find what pigeon-hole it really belongs to because it often reaches her in a fragmentary way. In terms of material information she may be quite at a loss at times to find that pigeon-hole. The listener can be equally puzzled; at other times, however, he understands very well. At times a dialogue leaves even a faithful medium puzzled. She is not given enough to understand the situation the other two are talking about and sharing. Sometimes this bye-passing is deliberate for it provides better evidence.

If information only comes in a fragmentary way, it is especially difficult for the medium to find the right context in which to put it. Bertha Harris once received such a fragment – one of redness and from a male communicator. She first said he had a red beard, but then went on to say: 'No, he lived at Redhill', which was correct. When a medium hears something apparently nonsensical she will want to suppress it as obviously wrong. She has to have the courage to speak out. Annie Brittain once heard 'A lawn made of turnip seeds'. She summoned her courage and relayed it and it turned out that this correctly described a practical joke the communicator had once played on the recipient, his brother, to whom he had purposely supplied the wrong seeds to lay a new lawn.

2

Unfortunately at the present time due to over-ready acceptance of diminished and insufficient standards, indifferent or poorly trained mediums considerably outnumber the more talented, and the very much smaller number of excellent ones who work less in terms of evidence, and more at what is better called soul level. It is easy for those who come with prejudiced intent to judge the whole mediumistic fraternity by the yardstick of the least successful practitioners. This is being deliberately unfair. The opposite prejudice results in foolish overpraise. One does not profitably judge the art of painting by the exhibits on park railings, or in the seaside shop.

At the simplest level of course are mediums who are content with everyday messages of a kind that any listener will understand. Communicators who then appear will probably be on not too distant a level from their listeners. This is usually called the astral field, and what is of value will be a degree of evidence of survival. This is not always as valid as supposed. If such a medium is pressed to give more, she will often be able to do no more than make general statements of doubtful validity produced from shop-soiled stock or perhaps mere guesses, wild or tame, material planted in very shallow soil. Simple near-at-hand evidence of survival is of more value than this.

Better evidence is often given which is highly particular to the recipient. Trivia can then often be of value, when not of an obvious kind, as when a listener was told of a bun-penny secreted well beyond sight on the top of a wardrobe, which was later found to be accurate. If a relation is claimed, never heard of by the listener and denied at the time but subsequently found to have existed, this is not water-tight evidence since we know little about the capacity of memory contents. If the communicator and the fact produced are both unknown, but prove when found later, to have important emotional consequences for the listener, this has a much greater degree of solidity. If some unknown fact or emotion is revealed which uncovers a painful episode or allows a relationship to be now understood, or which calls for a forgiveness never given on earth by the one concerned, we are coming nearer to the ground where an important change in a person's attitude and character can result from the message. Evidence grows in value the more deeply it touches something long buried in the listener's nature, perhaps a strong emotional flaw, or some unwarranted obstinacy of character.

Difficult blocks can lie in the communicator as much as the recipient, perhaps very difficult ones to speak of. Perhaps a confession is called for from one party and generosity from the other, or an attempt to right a wrong.

The basic value of this type of evidence depends upon the effects it subsequently produces. Does it lead to a remedy by which the true but damaged former relationship can be restored and renewed? Here we are moving again into the area of soul level and of interior spiritual growth.

It is only to be expected that a recipient in the early stages of investigation and of learning the best way to sit, will sometimes fall rather short in his understanding of what is happening at the medium's end. He cannot be expected to be fully sensitive to her professional difficulties.

It can well be asked whether there is not any way of lessening the all too frequent stumbling in medium and recipient alike. Why do not communicators do something to make things better? The answer is that they often do, though it must not be overlooked that many communicators are tyros, that they may be deep in emotion when making contact; also as said in Chapter Two very nearly all describe the process as difficult. It is likely that many fail and give up early or perhaps decide not to attempt it at all when as onlookers they witness communicator's words often going astray because the medium fails to understand the message, or her brain is set off in a wrong direction because some words produce mental and emotional associations of her own which the communicator is then unable to put right.

The principal and often very successful way of improving the situation and greatly clarifying it is a very simple one. It is, as said in Chapter Two, to accept help from someone experienced and quite at home in communicating, and who can be trusted to be largely accurate, much more so than the tyro communicator finds possible on his own.

These helpers, who give clear indication of having been trained for the task are known as 'controls' and offer a well-known and important route as an intermediary. The control becomes very used to the medium's way of working, and will be available to the same medium over a number of years. This is an obvious advantage.

The partnership, though familiar and well established, nevertheless has its delicate aspects. The control does not intrude, her task is to learn before the sitting what the communicator wishes her to say, and then to pass it on as objectively as she can. The other part of her task is to help to still the mind of the medium, and to secure her full attention, with as little deviation of meaning as possible. She also has to overcome occasional puzzlement, when the medium misunderstands what is intended and gives it another interpretation. An illustration – though in fact no control was involved at the time – is when Estelle Roberts, on the platform, said she had heard the word 'lie', and wondered if she was being asked to lie down. She went on to recognise that the reference was to a village, the name of which was spelt differently, but is pronounced as she had heard it.

The control when working is obliged to approach close to the medium's receptive 'antennae' and to overcome the sort of difficulties a communicator would have faced. A control does not lose her threads of attention, nor become muddled, nor break off as an early communicator often does. She also needs to discourage or prevent the medium jumping too soon at the meaning intended, or substituting platitudes of her own in place of the true message. A control has a valuable part to play, her established familiarity with the medium greatly helping all those concerned.

A control is not of the stature of a mentor, whose role is discussed later. A mentor is an altogether deeper being, though not too lofty to step in at times and take on the role of the control. Usually the control presents herself in a feminine aspect, though not always, and sometimes in a childlike presentation, though at times an adult sensibility and understanding are clearly present somewhere. Such a control can sometimes be very disarming by her friendliness to a rigid male recipient. It is difficult to form a true picture of a control. It will hardly be disputed that some use is made of the medium's natural earth temperament. It is perhaps best looked upon as a partial partnership. We still know little, however, of all the intricacies almost certainly involved behind the scenes.

The evidence given by a control is sometimes very compelling. It is easy to see that a young person's natural brightness of attention might pick up a message easily and accurately. Feda, the control of Gladys Osborne Leonard for many years, was presented as having lived as a Hindu girl. She was very useful in producing complex material, for instance in the exchange of information about communication processes, especially in the area of psychical research, between the Rev. Drayton Thomas, a Nonconformist parson, and his father who had also been a clergyman.

Equally Feda succeeded in producing helpful material as from F.W.H. Myers to the then living Oliver Lodge, and later in a long and important communication from Lodge after his death giving his views, some similar to his earth ideas and some changed, concerning what he had so far discovered since his death.

A control figure is undoubtedly a useful contributor to the mediumistic situation, but out of current favour with psychical researchers who are surely far from having exhausted this vein.

Of particular benefit are the control's qualities of willingness, and the accompanying accuracy and faithfulness it brings. These, as much as familiarity with the process, make the control a better communicator than the persons she serves are at all likely themselves to become. The control's extra qualities of character add a contribution which has the effect of sweetening the communication whilst still remaining entirely faithful to its purpose.

3

What then is mediumistic reception like, if it is different from earthly conversation? It often takes on a telepathic form; in our terms it is extrasensory rather than sensory. We can form an idea of what this is like when sometimes we sense the thoughts and feelings of another person. Though unspoken, they do not go unperceived. The impression reaches us in an interior and often unsought way. As with other frailties in human discourse it is not always received fully accurately: we intrude and impose, add or diminish. We can be imperfect witnesses even in reporting our own telepathic impressions to ourselves. We sometimes prefer to edit impressions to support existing prejudices.

A medium's impressions are usually mental or emotional. Some mediums, according to their power of visualisation, project the impression outwards, finding it easier to describe it in terms of an outward image. It is often easier to convey in this way but the primary impression has often welled up from a telepathic source and the medium then describes it in the way most natural to her. At other times, what is 'seen' is not the communicator himself but a picture projected by him on to the mind of the medium.

Such subtle telepathic reception often requires a degree of dissociation on the medium's part. The perception is at once fragile yet, to the medium, authentic. If a listener interrupts at an inappropriate instant or adds extra comments, it is very liable to snap the medium's own delicate telepathic thread, and often it is not easy for her to regain it.

Clearly a lot of goodwill and practice are necessary all round for the best results to be obtained. One is hardly likely to be able to get deeper into the minds of purported communicators unless one is willing in due time, tentatively at least, to drop suspicion and work realistically towards a working hypothesis of survival and to treat communicators provisionally as if they are what they claim to be.

Some mediums sense instantly what type of material it will be possible to give. Sometimes a medium will receive a familiar private symbol telling her the level at which she is to work. Perhaps she will be obliged to tune in to a more everyday step on the ladder of consciousness than with another client. The one in her presence will naturally remain unaware of this.

One medium, for instance, at times receives the image of a deep blue night sky filled with stars. This is her signal that she is to work at her deepest; it also intensifies the demands upon her sensitivity. Perhaps she will start at the top of this ladder of perception, and as the session proceeds, gradually tune down to more mundane communicators. Another medium will rely entirely on the guidance of her spiritual teacher, when he is one who prefers to take very full charge. For another, to do her best requires turning her attention fully away from her recipient. Her beam of attention will be deep and narrow, and to avoid the recipient's intrusion she keeps him away from her attention as best she can. Geraldine Cummins, who worked at a deep level, once said to a friend: 'I wish the blasted sitter was not there at all'. These differences of approach need to be respected, based as they are on the medium's own experience of how to use her gift at its most finely tuned. Then it can become very clear why it is not for the recipient to attempt to take control and direct the subject-matter. If he does he will almost certainly confuse the issue.

It is a fact that although the session normally comes about at the recipient's desire, and it is a service for which he is paying a professional fee, in reality he is very much the novice where the conduct of the proceedings is concerned. The degree of attunement the medium reaches is her concern, and indeed few recipients have anything but a very literal idea of what is taking place. It is assumed that the medium can turn her attention to any communicator on request but the medium often cannot by any means be fully her own mistress of ceremonies. In the main she is a passive instrument, her obedience as fully disciplined as she can make it. A communicator's difficulties include sometimes becoming scared at first by a constrictive, imprisoning dulling-down sensation. A price of some sort has to be paid by a communicator who has to accept limitations he cannot overcome; many complain particularly of the clumsiness they now find in words for what they want to convey. A communicator usually improves as he becomes accustomed to the difficulties but clearly he is obliged to compromise and sometimes probably is obliged to leave out what he most wants to say.

INNER EYE, LISTENING EAR

Most mediums, as said, are helped by at least a bare assurance that they are on the right track. It is not encouraging to be met with total silence. We have seen that sometimes they have to present their material in a void without any accompanying context. It is difficult then for a medium to know whether indeed it does relate to the recipient at all. If a medium is somewhat in the dark, a recipient's honest response is beneficial; it spurs and warms the medium's intention, but the response must be without intrusion, and needs to be brief.

A good medium has a very great respect for the intention of a communicator as serious as herself; she puts herself fully at his or her service. What results then can best be described as a brotherhood of the heart. The recipient is invited to share it.

At other times mediums find themselves forced to work at the level introduced or insisted upon by a leaden, or obstinate recipient, or, in a church, by the general level of the congregation. There is a real predicament here. For most sensitives it would be too difficult or too exhausting to raise up the very drab level around her, whilst at the same time having to remain in tune with the brighter and more subtle level of her communicator. Some mediums, more martial in temperament, can by their forthrightness do something to raise the level, whilst other equally good sensitives would be defeated. At a private session Mrs Sharplin, a well-known medium, would take a different stand. Her guide, in trance, would say: 'We will speak to you, since you wish it, about your relatives, but first you must allow us to speak of spiritual things'. A spiritually-oriented medium will always aim to be in obedience and harmony with her own mentor. For her, this underlies all, and is an essential part of her dedication. Any medium obviously can at times become close to the border of allowing her own temperament to intervene and provide an interpretation in tune more with herself. This is one way in which material takes on colouration from the medium. In the simplest terms, the motherly type of medium is likely to produce an over-comfortable message which the recipient feels he must considerably discount. An independent-minded and detached masculine medium, on the other hand, will probably concentrate on a more factual or intellectual message; there is nothing motherly about him, so that motherly aspects in the communicator largely pass him by. He does not record them because they are of no real interest to him.

The level at which a session takes place is partly determined then by the medium, partly by the communicator, partly by the recipient. If they have different ideas about it, the results will suffer. That is why it is so important for harmony to come about between all three, and this can often take quite a number of sessions to achieve, and calls for humility and patience.

It is obvious that by its very nature, some of the best information given for the recipient to assess is likely to hold meanings special to him; it relates to his own inner experience and his estimate cannot wholly be set aside only because it is subjective. He necessarily is closest to it, whether his powers of judgment are good or poor. This matters less with straightforward things, but the message may treat of things other than the everyday. It may relate, for instance, to moral or religious experience, or to a key fact of a private kind in the recipient's life pattern. Whatever his assessment, he is best sited to make it. After all, it has in the past happened, or is now happening, to him.

In mediumship, as in many things, the good is the enemy of the best, and the indifferent is the enemy of the good. Indifference to quality is the real enemy within the ranks, and is too often and too easily both offered and accepted.

4

A medium cannot break off to explain her processes to the sitter, least of all at that moment of inner concentration. The impressions reach the medium in waves, and she is not necessarily able to obtain extra telepathic information she would like to, or which is asked for. She is dependent upon her communicator's choice of material, as well as upon his ability to convey it. Thus she is often obliged to build up a picture gradually, and it will not necessarily be in temporal or logical order. The sitter too must wait and allow the picture to build up, and if he does ask, as he often does, for extra information, or information relating to a different subject matter or a different part of the communicator's earth life, he is unlikely to receive it. He must be patient. Much of a recipient's task lies in the art of listening. If the material appears fragmentary this impression may be removed in time. The attentive listener will also detect brief and telling sentences, which convey more in an instant than ten minutes of plodding recall. A less attentive listener can miss a nugget of this kind.

The medium will be nearer to her material on some days than on others, and feel more in tune. Obviously too she will work better for some sitters than others. As one clairaudient medium put it: 'Some days I "hear" exactly what is said, but on others I am only able to give the general sense of it in my own words'. The weather, her mood of the day, the degree of nervous energy she has available, and especially her harmony, or the reverse, towards her sitter can all influence the success of the séance.

Since she is largely dependent both on the communicator, and upon a number of earth factors she cannot fully control, on some days there will be an element of snatch-crop in what she produces, whilst on other days when harmony prevails, the stream will flow easily and often more deeply. True mediumship will then come about copiously. Here the communicator imparts, the medium absorbs, and the sitter responds, all in harmony with one another.

A recipient often comes determined to contact one

particular communicator, and will not accept others, or only grudgingly. Such an occasion is doomed to failure, since it goes right against the necessity of leaving the conduct of the sitting to be decided at the discarnate end. It is from there that it will be more easily seen what it is possible and desirable to give.

If the recipient takes into his own hands the asking of questions, often on matters quite separate from what has so far been produced, this is highly likely to bring about what a very experienced researcher has called 'awakening the mind of the medium', who in her partly dissociated state will wish to respond, but having had her link disturbed is liable unconsciously to conjure up an answer from herself. Again the sitter will have introduced confusion at a moment when the medium most needs silence to establish or deepen her link.

One medium might decide for herself how much at a deeper level her recipient can accept. Another might try to help where she felt a true spiritual need of which her client is as yet largely unaware. But such decisions in a spiritually-oriented medium would always be looked for by her in obedience to and in harmony with her own mentor. This would underlie all.

5

When evidence of survival is at a near-earthly level it is the recipient who normally judges the accuracy, but contradictory judgments can arise if the medium happens to be a better judge of the material than the recipient. The recipient can interpret mistakenly just as the medium can. He can also be restless and inadequate in his level of attention. Some mediums, as we have seen in Geraldine Cummins, find the best working stance is to divert as much of their attention as they possibly can away from the recipient. Then an intensely directed focus of attention helps to produce a deep level of material.

Using an Army term, it is all too easy an option for a medium to include commonality items. A commonality spare part is one which will fit many different makes of vehicles: a commonality message is general enough to apply to many people and even if true is thus of little or no value as evidence.

Reception by the medium, then, is by no means as straightforward as the average listener supposes. A medium sometimes 'hears' words but 'hears' them silently as in private thought. For others, a sentence can convey itself not in a succession of words, but as an instant whole. At other times a thought is known to be there, or known to be around, and is felt to be valid, even though as yet its right formulation has not found expression – there is a blurring in perception. These more subtle modes are how some mediums pick up much of their information. They have to depend upon a kind of inner impact, it might be called a form of osmosis. As the medium Stephen O'Brien has put it 'all spirit communication ... occurs within the mind' and more precisely still the medium Eileen Roberts says 'We "see" them not with our physical eyes but with our consciousness, our mind'. But that is not the end of the matter.

To illustrate, let us say that a medium senses a communicator as wearing a shawl. The medium may not be able to describe its colour or pattern, yet the basic fact is accurate. She does not see the shawl, she just 'knows' it. It is then likely to tell her something else, perhaps indicate the era when the communicator lived, when it was common to wear a shawl. Still no shawl is actually seen, what we have is likely to be a thought-picture projected by the lady who once owned the shawl. Such a perception, so far, is obviously incomplete, and here the medium needs to rely on the most basic part of all her training (if it has been good training) which is by long and faithful practice to know exactly what she has received, and,

THE MEDIUM AT WORK: EARLY LEVELS

except when the discretion of wisdom is needed, to repeat it without adding or subtracting from it in the very slightest. If she fails her training, she at once becomes open to any amount of error. Thus, just because the communicator wore a shawl, the medium might go on to describe her as elderly. In fact, she might have worn the shawl because she was delicate and died as a young woman. If the medium refuses to deviate from her primary perceptions, this leaves the way open for her to go back to the communicator, and to seek further and perhaps more significant evidential facts. Possibly the recipient inherited the shawl. If sensed as a Paisley shawl, this might only be a way for the communicator to convey that she was a Scot.

Alternatively, the initial sensing of the shawl could be intended as a symbol, to convey a particular meaning or emotion of which the medium may not, and sometimes need not, be fully aware. A fragmentary message when the medium is truly attuned, can sometimes be very significant to the recipient, though the medium may not know in what way. The communicator may be trying to convey by the symbol of the shawl that the listener is in need of some particular protection. The medium might then sense the communicator as taking off the shawl and draping it round the listener. The listener in turn may know exactly what this act is intended to tell her. Sometimes, of course, a lazy or over-eager medium can add a faulty interpretation just because it seems plausible.

If she refrains, and does not spoil the message, it may then reinforce a further intuitive impression of her own. Or, though more seldom, and at risk, the listener herself adds a confirming fact to the message and may do so accurately. But her own intuition might not have arisen if the medium had not spoken first, and behind the medium is also the communicator's urgency to reinforce it.

On particularly favourable occasions, the medium produces a cluster of facts, impressions and emotions, each leading to and relevant to the next, and at its best a highly accurate telepathic relaying of a complex message, combining several emotional levels. When this occurs, it will be from a medium who knows when to let things alone. At the same time neither the medium nor the recipient can be expected altogether to desert their own temperament. This can help sometimes but hinder at others. The overbearing and intrusive medium can destroy or prevent what could have been the most important part of the intended communication. So unfortunately can the overbearing, fearful or negative recipient. Some wilfully close their ears, and deny what they know to be true. Some mediums too, as in any profession, only possess a selection of the full skills available.

Apart from the quality of the evidence given, one or two simple factors indicate poverty of material in the session. The first is when a medium produces a long string of Christian names, nearly all of which the sitter does not recognise. This is a sure indication that the medium is out of tune. Since some of the names will be common ones, a sitter is likely to know some relatives or friends to whom they might apply, but when he claims them, any succeeding information will be fragmentary, irrelevant, or plain wrong.

Another sign is when a correct name and information are given but nothing new to the recipient is transmitted, and any message will be so obvious as to be nearly meaningless, or little more than a trail of useless platitudes. At such a session the medium will hop about from one communicator to another, unable to hold any of them for more than a couple of minutes. At the opposite end of the scale is the much rarer medium who can hold the same communicator for the whole hour of the session, and can do so similarly for half a dozen sessions or more, from the same communicator, producing fresh information on each occasion.

It is necessary to estimate the depth, or otherwise, at which a medium is working. This can vary almost momentarily, between one part of the session and another. Some trance controls choose to give everyday material at first, because their hold upon the medium is still slender, and they will give the serious part of what they wish to say, perhaps one third of the way through, when they have stilled the medium's mind to the greatest extent possible. In trance one well-known teacher would produce his oration in a very steady and orderly way, then five minutes before the end, the medium would gently begin to snore, whilst still continuing the oration. The snoring, of course, indicated the gradual return of the everyday part of the medium's consciousness and the equally gradual loosening of his hold by the trance control. Some controls of trance mediums prefer to produce the important part of their message right away whilst the medium is fresh. Each manages the situation in his own way. Perhaps a useful image is that of a staircase, with several steps upon which the communicator chooses, or is able, to stand.

The medium's performance, especially that of beginners, is limited in another way. When she talks on without a break, it may be because if she does not do so she knows she will lose her hold. So she cannot let go in order to check with the sitter whether she is on a right course. Perhaps a medium is more concerned with her reputation, or her self-approval rather than with her sitter. Another medium, finding herself short of material, may unfortunately resort to a sly inspection of her sitter's costume and jewellery for clues. Better mediums would of course scorn to do this. Another will obtain nearly the whole of her material by telepathy from the sitter's own outer aura, not venturing sufficiently into the field of true communication. Such a medium operates as little more than a mirror of her sitter, and the sitter may give to it an altogether unsuitable authority, especially if he hears what he hopes to hear. Other mediums, particularly those whose main work is on the platform rather than with the private client, will sometimes go on insisting they are correct, even when the sitter continues to deny it. Platform mediumship indeed has its temptations, and it makes more difficulties when in such cases the medium is wrong nine times, but perhaps correct – as the sitter subsequently discovers or remembers – in the tenth fact.

It is hoped that these few notes will illustrate a little of the complex relationship between medium, communicator and recipient as they begin to explore the demands made by each upon the other.

Sometimes – and this is where a very careful choice arises – a medium perceives it will be both more intelligible and more acceptable readily to speak from her own wisdom, her own experience of life but she must then on no account let the client think the medium's own wisdom is discarnate wisdom. They can be closely intermeshed, but it does not at all do to present one as the other. This wisdom needs to be well chosen if it is to make an impact upon the particular client consulting her. It may also be imperfect and tainted. If she fails here to be very clear as to her ground, she is likely, sooner or later, to mislead both herself and her client and thus create a confusion.

A client will often look for a description of his communicator, largely made up of memories of his old life. The danger here is that whilst it may indeed be the communicator who is recounting his memories, at other times the medium can be drawing them from the client himself. She may in addition be drawing from, and reproducing the feeling tones in which these memories are embedded in her client. This danger is now becoming better recognised by mediums.

It can be difficult to decide where the evidence is really coming from when the medium perhaps is giving correct facts of character, correct memories, habits of speech. There is need for care and some experience before accepting what seems so evidential, so like the person once known on earth.

Hence an important distinction is needed to distinguish

between telepathy drawn at earth level and true communication. When a medium is telepathically tuning in only to a client's aura she is contacting a this-world consciousness, something of what her recipient carries around as part of his own memories, his own personal make-up, his emotional history. This is present within his aura even when unrelated to what he is thinking or feeling at this particular moment during the séance; at these times the communicator may not be present at all. There can be important differences between what a communicator was when on earth and what he now is. The best mediums are well aware of this troubling difficulty and are trained to distinguish the difference between authentic material, and telepathic facts only borrowed from the recipient.

When a sitter asks near-at-hand questions, 'Should I move house?' 'Where can I find a better job?', or even 'Should I leave my wife?' this unfortunately forms something of an invitation for an unwary medium to pick up from the aura of the questioner the answer hoped for, instead of direct material from a spirit communicator's own insight.

This outer auric reading arises, putting it briefly, when the attention of the medium is placed in the wrong area. Mediums who are well taught know the remedy is to stop and wait whilst attuning themselves once again into a deeper level.

At other times if a medium is working largely from the everyday part of herself, then she is likely to reach only communicators who have not yet cast off much of their earth ways. If communication can come about it is obviously possible to make contact with new arrivals and shallow and mischievous people, as well as with mature beings of insight and loving concern. The mere fact of communication obviously in no way guarantees depth. A rather odd fact, but not without its own humour, is that intellectual sitters sometimes get good results from a medium who can hardly put together a grammatical sentence. However, the feeling contents of the mediums' make-up can be richer and more accurate than their client's own perhaps somewhat impoverished ones and it is here that such mediums provide a valuable contribution.

At other times tuning in at telepathic level can result in a very accurate character reading of the sitter himself; but if it tells one no more than one already knows about oneself, of what value is it? If a medium is demonstrating her skills in this way, is she not merely giving a performance? That is not what her work is about.

One simple test of a session has always existed: to ask oneself at the end of it 'Do I know anything I did not know already?' If the answer is 'No', it is likely that much has been drawn from the client. Such sessions often produce a sense of disappointment which tells its own story. The situation is worse still when the client goes away buoyed up with hopes that all he has privately wished for will come about.

The difference between fortune-telling and prediction is subtle but important. Fortune-telling is useless and usually is drawn from, and deals only with, the client's own desires. Some sensitives, however, as Eileen Garrett did, achieve a special form of lucidity which extends both backwards and forwards into what lies on either side of the immediate present, and into the achieved past and indicated future. How can this lucidity properly be used? Eileen Garrett used it for character insight. It is then for the client to choose whether to do something towards altering himself. A simple gypsy, when genuine, can sometimes see a significant life event ahead, and may or may not interpret it aright. The importance of prediction lies in what use the recipient makes of it. Sometimes it is seen to have served as a warning when recalled later on, a warning which proves to have been needed.

Fortune-telling, on the other hand, is concerned with often illusory feelings and desires already sown in the client's own shallow ground. Prediction has to do with the raising of an

THE MEDIUM AT WORK: EARLY LEVELS

insight otherwise unavailable. It bears a serious meaning, or can do so.

Mediums who retain a fitting humility know that from one angle the client is the most important person at the séance. It is he and he only who, if he so chooses, can make use of the spiritual implications outlined, at the cost of overcoming something in himself or of growing a new quality. At times a sitting can have an aspect of the confessional, with the medium describing the sins rather than the penitent doing so, but again, it is the penitent who has to carry out the penance, which the mediumistic material may imply but certainly does not impose.

The basic situation is well summed up by Ivy Northage's mentor Chan:

> The auric levels on which most sensitives are working today will respond to the needs of the client on the level of emotional desire. You have an auric blending . . . if a sitter is full of her bereavement, it is very very easy on this auric level to be able to conjure up thought forms and emotional substitutions. And the mediums themselves are quite happy when the recipient says: 'Yes, he was exactly like that'; but it is no guarantee of the actual communication. Now your discrimination has to come from the mediums themselves. They would recognise, if they were knowledgeable, that they are getting it this way, and this of course would put them on their guard against any kind of promise or advice.
>
> We are making our special contribution to re-introduce and reinforce the importance of pure communication. It is infinitely more difficult when your medium is now in touch with the newly arrived spirit, with all the difficulties accompanying that spirit; it is not nearly as plain sailing as to say: 'He was like this, he was like that'.

Parallel to this, Trudy Brown's Chinese mentor has said in trance:

There are many people who think their problems are just of the world or their financial position, or their relationships, but of course these are only the leaves, the roots are of different magnitude. And so they see only that which is above the earth, and they say 'Well, my flower droops', or 'My leaves are not green because she does not love me', or 'Because I do not have a place to live', or 'Because my mother does not understand me'. It is of course little to do with that. And if your mediums can say: 'You do not get on with your husband, or your children, or your mother because of things wrong with them, but because you are viewing your life in the wrong way, because that which you have come to learn is not to do with having an easy relationship' . . . if your medium can say this to people then it will help them not only in their everyday relationships but with the understanding of their paths.

This is straight talk.

CHAPTER FOUR

THE RECIPIENT'S TASK AND RESPONSIBILITY

1

WE HAVE ALREADY seen that like most human activities mediumship is far from perfect. This is partly owing to the shared responsibilities involved. What forms the recipient's share of these responsibilities, his part in the threefold partnership? Let us try and look at his viewpoint, with apology for any repetitions involved.

A discarnate message is a delicate thing; an act of human communication of a difficult, precarious and incomplete kind, expressing a human relationship, often dear and important, or it can be the work of a spiritual mentor, speaking through an instrument who, however skilled, must nevertheless be accepted as an imperfect translator. The rapport is transient and subject to interruption. This cannot be completely guarded against, any more than the image on the television screen can avoid being shaken by atmospherics or a passing plane. Failures in the mechanics of transmission, or in the medium's own receptivity, are different from those which arise from the recipient's mind and feelings, his own 'atmospherics' within him. Yet he also has his true powers of sensing, deep in his inner self, which he gradually learns to use, and which are stimulated by the medium's own areas of spiritual perception.

So in every session a task and a duty places itself upon the recipient. He accepts, rejects and sometimes re-interprets the material. He brings already formed attitudes into the séance room, of which he may not be altogether conscious. How well will he use these in meeting challenging new concepts? How far is he willing gradually to alter what is wrong in himself? These are not light responsibilities.

After buying a ticket for an ocean cruise, and then reading the great amount of small print on the back, it becomes obvious that so many dreadful things could happen to the traveller for which the shipping company disclaims all liability that the only prudent course is to stay at home. Nevertheless one embarks on the journey. So with communication. Looking at the practicalities of this sometimes hazardous mental and emotional journey into the realm of the discarnate, let us concentrate on three factors on the recipient's side of the matter. First his technique, second, his quality of attention, and third the participation of his moral nature. Sitting with a sensitive is in its own way a skilled job; like other skills, it takes time and practice to achieve.

2

What technique is needed then?

Some enquirers expect something of a miracle, others attend convinced that nothing can happen. Obviously it is best to avoid these extremes and have an open and receptive attitude towards what comes. There is nothing magical or supernatural about it. He will be facing a complex act of human communication. The sensitive is trained to register impressions at a slightly more inward level of consciousness from those of everyday.

Her skills are like other professional skills, with the difference that mediumistic skills are rarer, and never wholly at the command of the person practising them; they are coloured to some extent by the medium's own mind. Nor can they be produced to order. The sensitive cannot be blamed for difficulties inherent in the nature of the communication process. Sensitives, too, are called on for varying tasks on which to concentrate. An enquirer should be clear whether it is evidence of survival which he requires, or spiritual advice, and it is wise to seek help in order to find a sensitive equipped to perform the task required.

In interviews with a sensitive the enquirer needs to recognise that even in silence he cannot avoid participating. This is still the case even if the listener considers himself a detached observer. His attitude helps to bring about good results, or to mar them, or even make them impossible.

Patience is needed as well as perseverance. If a discarnate communicator is present who has not used the process before, he or she too will need to learn. Or it may be that the listener will not feel in harmony with the medium or vice versa. This will make it harder for good results to come about.

If the first sensitive consulted is not the right one for him, then he needs to experiment with one or two others by a process of trial and error. He should not be discouraged by this. Every interview is to some degree an experiment. On the other hand if the results are satisfactory it is unwise to be too elated, but to take time, in the days following the interview to sift and analyse the results with care, asking oneself also how far one's own criteria are valid in this context.

At the séance do not talk or comment more than is barely essential. Apart from giving away evidence, which it invariably does if only by inference, any sort of running commentary only distracts the medium who is doing all she can to place her attention elsewhere. The medium is trying to paint a verbal picture. It does not do for the recipient to paint his own idea of the scene on top of hers. He does not yet know its true design nor what is going to be added to what has so far been given.

INNER EYE, LISTENING EAR

Some readers will remember the early cat's whisker wireless sets, when a good contact would suddenly come and as suddenly go. It is rather the same with mediumship. The threads which reach her are very delicate, so are not always grasped aright. One of the listener's tasks then is to decide if the medium is on the wrong track. Occasionally it can prove later on that the medium was right after all. Or the medium can be basically in possession of true facts, which have been interpreted awry, or put into an incorrect context.

The next factor in building up a good technique is to appreciate that one statement neither guarantees nor falsifies another. If statement A, claiming to come from a communicator is correct, it does not mean that statement B must be. Nor if statement B proves wrong does it always infer that statement A did not come from the communicator at all. It may, it may not. A perfectly genuine communicator may get off the beam, and later succeed in getting on to it again. So the sitter has to be very honest in sorting out the wheat from the chaff, neither self-indulgent when deciding in favour, nor equally self-indulgent through being over-ruthless in deciding against it. It follows that a number of items will have at times to be placed in a mental 'suspense tray', to see whether later on they are corroborated or not, perhaps in future sittings after many months. The 'suspense tray' calls for patience, and is a very necessary and valuable part of the recipient's equipment. He has constantly to deal with probabilities rather than certainties, and whichever side of the scales his estimate tips down, he has to watch out against becoming too certain too soon.

'But I must check up' says the recipient, naturally enough. To do so he begins to ask questions. This again calls for a self-denying ordinance. Important though it is to try and obtain assurance, this is usually not the way to do it. It is therefore essential to remain flexible, and not to expect and certainly not to insist upon material being too cut and dried. The communicator with his difficulties often cannot comply with the sitter's requests, even if he wishes to. Such requests sometimes only increase the difficulties. He does not have as much command for the situation as may appear. If the recipient in his anxiety not to be deceived, tries to usurp the initiative and ask for more information, he is likely to be disappointed.

Communicators too say there are spiritual laws they must obey, which govern what they are allowed to tell, and what must be left for the recipient to find from his own experience. Some go to a medium hoping for a crib which will gain them some material or even financial advantage, but this will not be found. The only sensitive I know of who decided to use her gift in the stock market became, and long remained, an undischarged bankrupt. Spiritual advantage is highly unlikely to be gained if unearned. Half-baked information confidently claimed as a pearl of wisdom discredits recipient and medium alike.

It needs to be repeated that the client who leaves the choice of material to the communicator will in the end be the gainer. If it offends his self-assertion or his avidity for more and more details, he will learn by experience that the best and most unexpected evidence comes to the recipient who is patient. Communication, like politics, is the art of the possible.

It can be seen that there is a difference between the checking-up type of questions, only designed for gently smoothing out uncertainties in material already given, and intrusive questions, either introducing new themes altogether, or cross-examining rather than elucidatory. Questions which are too intrusive, can push the medium's suggestibility into directions not intended by the communicator. Then the medium can unconsciously mirror the sitter's own mind, and both sitter and medium may mistake it for the communicator's. The medium's mind can sometimes be like a bolting horse, and the only reins the communicator has are cotton ones; in this situation it does not help if the sitter whips up the horse. Hence the need for stillness and peace.

Perhaps this suggestibility brings on at times what might be called a 'Mrs Blarney' in some mediums, operating below fully conscious level. She wants to do her best for her client, and if he asks too pressing questions it is sometimes Mrs Blarney who colours the answers. Even when questions are invited by the medium towards the end of the session, as they frequently are, it is often wise to limit them, and often better still not to ask them at all.

To give an example of a common type of misunderstanding the communicator begins giving, one by one, the facts he has come with; he starts off, perhaps, with his Christian name. As the first few facts are given the recipient starts fitting them into his own framework of memory; if the name say of Richard is given he thinks or says 'Oh, my brother', and starts applying subsequent statements as if from his brother. But it may be the wrong framework; it may be another Richard altogether. The listener who thus jumps the gun can soon introduce confusion into a situation already difficult enough. He can follow false trails without recognising that he has himself started them. He needs to be ready to come back to the original starting point. This is a very necessary point of technique.

Then too the recipient sometimes needs the shifting perceptions, the assimilation of small hints, called for in good conversation. So also does the medium in listening to her communicator. After all a sitting, in spite of the difficulties, is also a social occasion, and the communicator is hoping to make it an important and significant one. To sum up in a sentence, listening is best done in as selfless a way as possible, so as to be as sure as one can of what the communicator is really attempting to say. To put it more briefly: be inwardly still, listen, and learn not to intrude.

3

The second factor – and these factors are of course interlocking ones and cannot completely be separated – is the *quality of attention* given. There are subtle ways in which a sitter deeply influences things; where his mind is every bit as real a factor as if it were a physical presence.

Many difficulties confronting mediums are caused by the recipient, but are often entirely unrealised by him, for naturally enough many recipients know very little about the complexities of transmission. This is only to be expected in earlier sessions, though unfortunately it often continues for long afterwards.

A central difficulty lies in the medium having to perform a double task, that of listening inwardly very deeply and quietly in order to obtain her material, and then instantly passing it on in such a way as to make recognised both its surface meaning and also, if possible, the deeper import it sometimes bears. In order to do this she often needs to switch her level of attention. Her material, as we have seen, often first comes to her in a fragmentary way without any surrounding context. If, for instance, the medium senses, or sees, or smells violets, she may not know at first whether this relates to a Christian name, a time of the year, an event such as a gift, or a symbol. The medium must not guess nor jump the gun; she must wait for what comes to her by going back to the communicator. Whilst this delicate process is taking place, since the transmission can fade at any moment the medium usually tries to hand on the first piece of her material to the recipient at once in case she loses it; having thus anchored it she can then let it go, and concentrate inwardly once more.

It is here that the inexperienced or insensitive recipient needs to accept the material quietly, and avoid comments which can pull the attention of the medium away from where it needs to be. The recipient only needs to be neutral in a quiet and friendly way, and leave the next step to the medium. As the picture is built up he can say when appropriate 'Yes I understand' or 'That is meaningful' or 'Please continue with that'. It helps a medium to know she is on the right track, but she does *not* wish to know in what way she is right, except from her own sources. If at first the recipient cannot connect, or is not sure if the medium is right or wrong, it is sometimes best to remain peacefully silent for a moment or two, thus permitting the medium to add further and perhaps decisive details.

It is said on earth in many context that you get what you pay for. There can of course also be an element of gift, the unexpected and perhaps undeserved bestowal; both these elements are sometimes present for a recipient. Most often the quality of his attention determines what will come to him. The quality of the medium also comes into it. A good medium will nearly always do better for a poor recipient than a poor medium can do for a good recipient. As so often in the human situation, with all its individual permutations and combinations, rules cannot be too hard and fast; but they can point correctly to general tendencies. Largely by the company he keeps in the séance room – the communicators who reach him – a recipient can recognise something of his own standing.

In general a recipient is not anything like as passive as he should be. Instead he brings his own demands and expectations; seeking to contact the communicator he most wants, rather than the one who is waiting to come, and requiring, or even virtually demanding, confirmation on matters on which he has often already made up his own mind. The wishes and doubts and confusions strewn over his untidy personal life are likely to be his main concern. Probably he is much less keen about the spiritually oriented pathway which a long-experienced mentor sees he is intended to take and towards which he steadily points. A communicator who claims attention may have died only recently, and, speaking at much the same spiritual level as the recipient, is unlikely to be able to bring deep help. In spite of death, he can still be as spiritually confused as the recipient, although both may think otherwise. Nevertheless bereavement and accompanying doubt and fears and longings in the recipient can attract real help, sometimes at more than a simple level. To reach conviction that those he loved have survived death and can speak to him is of great importance to him. It is an individual matter; evidence which satisfies one will pass another by as useless or irrelevant. A communicator soon after death can be as overcome with emotion as the recipient, and then the message intended fails to get through fully.

If, apart from necessary evidential discretion, the recipient is fundamentally unwilling within himself to acknowledge either privately or publicly any value in the material he is about to receive, he is introducing a deadening influence into his session. In a subtle way the sensitive will feel the obstruction, and that the recipient is not going to stand by the truth in the session, and this will discourage her and perhaps baffle her. The over-eager client, on the other hand, tends to sophisticate the material in favour of his own expectations. The tape recorder often shows that things which were genuinely believed to have been said were not really said at all. I regret to say I have fallen into this trap.

Many mediums, although they may not like to admit it, can find the recipient's presence more harmful than helpful. Some, however, welcome the opportunity of asking whether they are right or wrong, and can do so at a moment when their attention is not linked elsewhere. However, when the medium becomes aware of a waiting presence – to use a crude analogy, rather like a silent telephone ring if one can imagine such a thing – it can then be very distracting if the recipient insists on continuing to speak at that moment.

INNER EYE, LISTENING EAR

The recipient is required to learn from his innate discretion, or from former experience, remembering always that his function is to receive, and not to direct or demand.

Let us say that the medium has produced two or three facts which fit together and the recipient has found this meaningful and has accepted it, then the medium is ready to move on to further information, probably with growing confidence. This material may be trivial, or deeply meaningful. If the first, the triviality may be due to the communicator who has died too recently to have anything really worthwhile to impart. Or it may be due to the medium; if she is comparatively undisciplined and of somewhat shallow nature her own lines of communication can be very short. Every medium has natural limits of sensitivity and understanding. Communicators, however, on rare occasions overcome these limits, and succeed in putting through, probably in a few words and often in a wrapped-up form, something which can give the recipient an important key for the next part of his life. Usually, however, the medium will work within her normal range.

As further material is built up, the recipient will have more difficulty in keeping to his original role, but it remains essential that he should not try to divert the material to what *he* thinks the meaning is. It may be quite different from what he is expecting; the whole point can be that it is so. Even for the seasoned recipient it can be surprisingly easy to fall into this error. The message then begins to get off course, and continues to do so further, rather like a branch railway line which gradually draws further and further away from the main line. It can then be hard for the communicator to restore the material to the right direction.

On her side, the medium does have a little latitude; she can, if she thinks fit, question her communicator silently about what he is trying to say, for she, of course, can jump the gun just as a recipient often does. But the medium also senses

THE RECIPIENT'S TASK AND RESPONSIBILITY

much sooner when an error is arising. She can ask, or send out a mental request for the original impression to be repeated, maybe in an altered form. Just as the recipient needs to be obedient in the right way, so also do both communicator and medium.

The most common mistake made by the recipient, as said earlier, lies in supposing the communicator simply speaks and the medium merely relays the words. Would that mediumship were so simple! It is better recognised as a process in which the mental and feeling world of the communicator touches upon the fringes of the mental and feeling world of the sensitive. Putting it in another way, the communicator influences the inner aura of the medium and then aims at imparting into it something of his own quality, so that if only briefly, the two are very much in tune. During the more rarefied atmosphere at these moments the medium has, at her end, to gather the message intended, in terms of the communicator's perception rather than her own. If the recipient intrudes at such a delicate moment, he will shatter the link and the medium, bruised in her sensibility, will need to start all over again.

During the sensing process, whatever the level reached, the medium's antennae of perception, which in normal living are kept within and guarded securely, will be extended outwards and her entire aura will become open, not only to the delicate inner indications she is seeking, but also to the much coarser impressions of the outer world. That is why, during a session, even quite a slight move on the recipient's part can startle the medium, and even a small sound can be very disturbing. Even in her ordinary non-working times a medium can occasionally find her aura invaded by some person of coarse sensibility near her. She might then perhaps feel herself obliged to get off a bus – as Walter de la Mare once had to – because of the unpleasant impact of a nearby passenger. It is no easy thing for a medium to live unguarded in the world, and if her aura is left open for too long, the result is a draining away of a good deal of her nervous energy; she will both feel and be depleted or exhausted. To lesser degree this can happen also to normally sensitive persons in ordinary life.

4

What of the large proportion of enquirers who come with a deep emotional desire to discover the presence of someone dearly loved? This strong emotion may operate towards over-credulity; or exactly the opposite, a great reserve, and determination not to be misled, and a wholly proper hesitation in yielding to that interior conviction, that quiet endorsement from within which is the reward of communications which ring true for both medium and receiver.

Such an enquirer's task, however urgent the emotion, often calls for a period of apprenticeship, to learn at first-hand some at least of the difficulties and limitations inherent in third-party mediumship. This is probably why at first a less important, even seemingly irrelevant communicator turns up, to the eager recipient's disappointment. The final prize can be great, and worth the patience needed.

At the opposite pole, some create barriers through demanding to be convinced, yet at the same time refusing the responsibility of reaching a conviction through their own sensibility and judgment. At a more subtle level some enquirers come in emotional and intellectual fear, yet always refusing this proper responsibility of decision: divided and unhappy, they pass from one medium to another. The experienced observer comes to know their difficulty, but it is extremely hard for them to recognise that the barrier is really in themselves.

In the case of some research sitters the more sternly and strictly objective these set out to be, the more easy it seems to be to overlook themselves as an important subjective factor in the situation. There is a kind of sceptic – he is recognised on sight – who has a withering effect on the receptivity of the medium, and yet remains curiously indifferent to what he thus carries around with him. Very different is the sitter – also well-known – who starts by saying 'I am afraid I am extremely critical', and then straight away demonstrates his credulity. Another well-known character is the butterfly listener who hangs on the medium's lightest word, and next week goes on to hang on some other medium's lightest word, but never stops still long enough to take in what any medium really did say. There are, too, emotionally dishonourable people who intend to do something they know to be wrong, and come determined to get the medium to say it is right. To quote a bare-faced example: most sensitives encounter from time to time a client who seeks approval for a love affair she anyhow intends to start. She may begin by asking about twin souls. On one occasion it went like this: 'Can you assure me my husband is going to die within the next twelve months?' That client wanted absolution, not advice. If a medium is bludgeoned like that, how can the delicate threads of true communication assemble themselves? And, if they do, will such a questioner listen? These types of client make up the misfits of the séance room.

To turn to quite a different aspect of the recipient's influence, some of his feelings whilst in the séance room are highly likely to transmit themselves to the medium. If a recipient catches himself feeling bored or disappointed he should try instead to give fresh and eager attention to each sentence spoken. This helps to preserve the medium's own freshness of tone, and will increase her alertness and her wish to work well. Suspicion causes a medium's antennae to droop, or even to draw in completely, and so does a cold expectation that the medium will have nothing worth while to impart. In the difficult context of psychic communication a fair hearing

INNER EYE, LISTENING EAR

calls for sympathy during the event *and judgment only afterwards*. The occasion is best approached in a friendly team-spirit, for the carrying-out of an experiment with a mutual purpose. That is what it is. These are the simple good manners of the séance room.

Now at times both care and sympathy are required in order to grasp the imagery correctly, and to recognise its correct scale of value. In conscious mediumship the sensitive may use homely language in a spiritual context, or vice-versa. In trance, on the other hand, as in dreams, the imagery may be over-vivid, more than life-size. To illustrate: some trance mediums need to drink water beforehand; on one occasion the control said his medium's body was short of water, and the trance ended prematurely. As the medium came round she said: 'I saw two huge negroes, and they picked me up and plunged me into a bath of water'. There surely you have imagery saying in an over-emphatic way only that the medium needed another glass of water! On another occasion, ten years ago, a control said to me: 'In the listening will come the answer'. That does not sound very much, but it has been of very great help to me ever since, and has unlocked many intuitions I would probably otherwise have lost. The second instance was as much under-scale as the first was over-scale. The recipient has to recognise the true scale. This side of the subject has been little studied.

Only by practice, by the recipient as well as the medium, can communication be improved. As with horses or motorcars, experience and experiments improve the breed. Every recipient who disentangles a difficulty is helping his successors. Ideally the qualities a recipient needs are to be as sympathetic as a hostess, as intuitive as an artist, as impartial as an historian, as fair as a judge. This you may say is indeed bringing up heavy artillery to assess what sometimes turns out to be very trivial information. True it may be trivial, but when it is otherwise it can arrive unexpectedly, and the listener needs to be ready. Amidst inconsequential material there can quite suddenly be produced what a purported discarnate Oliver Lodge called 'good ear of wheat'. The listener has to keep his attention alert, without himself adding too extravagant an interpretation. This calls for restraint of judgment.

At a deeper level the Delphic Oracle offers an interesting parallel to modern discarnate communication. The Delphic messages were sometimes ambiguous, and had to be interpreted. The famous message given at Delphi to King Croesus on the eve of battle, when he enquired the outcome, was: 'Next day a great Kingdom will fall'. The king proceeded to battle with good heart, but it was his own kingdom that fell. Was the advice no more, as rationalists say, than an odds-on bet, since whoever won, a kingdom was likely to fall? But when we enter the sphere of the numinous, of voices of mysterious authority, rationalists may well overlook the heart of the matter if they say that the priests merely interpret knowledge they had gathered skilfully from their own network of information.

It is germane to ask as well what attitude Croesus himself – the recipient so to speak – brought to his question, and still more pertinently, brought to his own interpretation of what was given to him. Surely he brought to it his own hubris, that overweening confidence which the Greeks recognised so well as their national vice; did not his hubris cause him to choose the one interpretation and overlook the other? In short what brought on the King's own doom was not the message, but how he read it. Was this the very thing the message was intending to warn him about? If so, it might be said that as a recipient he proved unworthy of his message. In the ambiguity lay the touchstone intended by the Oracle. The King interpreted wrongly, because he was wrong in himself. He neglected too the pregnant words of advice on the threshold at Delphi: 'Nothing too much'. Instead, he made his message support his own excess of hubris.

Discarnate messages can sometimes have, like the Oracle, this numinous element of coming from the dead. This makes it easy to yield up to them a wrong kind of authority, or transfer the words to a different context, perhaps a material realm to which they do not truly belong. No authority whatever lies in a statement merely because it comes from the dead. To be blunt: once careful interpretation is neglected the result is likely to be superstition. In the séance room today there is need to remember the Delphic injunction of 'Nothing too much' if the twin traps of superstition and misinterpretation are to be avoided.

So much for quality of attention. To try to sum it up. As at Delphi the listener judges the situation, but is also judged by it, and at times may fail it.

5

The third and most difficult theme concerns the engagement of the enquirer's moral nature in the situation.

Much communication, as all know, is at a comparatively shallow level. It often comes about on the recipient's side, because there is insufficient willingness to allow any deep commitment to arise. The communicator's side if it is to be dynamic, must express, and gradually transfer, a set of values. It this is to happen the communicator, at whatever level, must first have lived those values, must have made them his own; he also needs to have a measure of love for the recipient, personal or impersonal. That is his qualification in true communication. The recipient, of course, on his side must not leave all the responsibility to the communicator; he needs to build up within himself an area of response, a resonance, a bell which is in tune, a sounding-board, by which to judge. By learning the use of such a sounding-board the fruits of the communications gradually take on life, if the recipient is willing that they should, until in time he makes these fruits a true part of himself. It begins to be possible to listen also for the overtones in the communicator's words, and to value-impressions which sometimes convey themselves without words; this can happen equally well during the recipient's private analysis after the session. That is why it is most necessary to make a transcript from the tape-recording and sometimes meditate sentence by sentence on the parts – it will only be parts – which seem worthy of this. At first the sounding-board may fail to pick up these overtones and value-impressions, but it comes in time. In meditation, one's deeper communicators often succeed in passing their impressions to the person on earth via what psychologists call the deep centre, the senior partner of the daily self. More and more people are likely to become familiar with this process. Let us not limit the possibilities of communication to the séance room, taking it for granted that the help of a third party, the medium, is always necessary, however valuable such help can be.

In one way, communication can be said to provide a crutch, but it can be a crutch which in time can enable the recipient to walk better than before. Gradually through more and more skilled use of his own sounding-board he learns to find out the truths of his own nature. In this particular version – which of course is only one version – of the psychological transforming process, and aided by the help of a sensitive, a link can then be made with a kindly instructor, a mentor, who gently reintroduces one to neglected aspects of one's self. As the sounding-board is perfected, the mentor does not disappear, but works more from within, and is found there more readily by the pupil. A kind of interior telepathic dialogue can then arise. But if the pupil thinks to do without his teacher altogether, is he not returning, in part, to the egoism and separation of the lower self? Each man, my particular mentor has said, finds his own way back to God, with help.

INNER EYE, LISTENING EAR

Even with help it is his *own* way; true help is not a substitution, nor is it continuous. One can do without the help of mediums, of course, but in the end to refuse all help at any level, including interior levels, is surely to deny the oneness of spiritual life. Does it matter if the thought is one's own or another's as long as it is right and that now is the right time to know it and live it?

The question for the recipient, not to put too fine a point upon it, is how far can that which is imperfect in himself adversely influence this delicate relationship? He will gradually assess his communicator by the value-judgments implied in what the latter says. But suppose the recipient resists these stubbornly, because they conflict with value-judgments of his own he desires to continue to hold, and which probably are much more comfortable to hold? How far is he disinterested, how far does he welcome the truth of the situation; is he indeed seriously enough concerned about it? He may not want the truth; he may go further and try to force it into his own direction. It is not easy, even for a disciplined person, to absorb fully what a senior communicator really is attempting to say, not just 50% or 75% of it but as near to 100% as any imperfect human being can get. Unfortunately too, the communicator's meaning, as reported, may well be not so clear to a recipient handicapped by a degree of self-indulgence which clogs up his insight; or there may be some confusion about the intended area of reference, but if so, it is no good just preferring to believe it must refer to the area one wants it to refer to.

Another challenge arises when the communicator focusses on a blind spot in his listener. Nothing is harder to estimate correctly, after all, than one's faults and virtues; it is so easy to take the one for the other. Communication must not be limited to virtues and praise if there is to be the basis for a good rapport, to obtain which a listener must bring to the encounter as much of his real self as he can find. This is as hard as it sometimes is in the intimacies of human relationships on earth. The benefit of the situation is that in many cases the communicator has moved on further than the recipient and as a result is able more easily to be himself.

Discarnate instruction tells that each layer of consciousness, whether that of communicator or of his pupil here, remains dependent to some extent upon communion with the layer next above it. Like ourselves, the teacher has the joy of reaching up and imparting what is mediated from a layer above his own. To abandon old set beliefs of the personal earthly self is to make way for the inner self to discover and accept companions of the spirit whom the earthly self was never able to find. However it is very necessary here not to become too dependent upon others.

In accounts of life after death, it is clear that the whole of the former daily self does not travel on into heavenly spheres; on the contrary, much is gradually discarded and disappears. And when that has come to pass, whatever new things come to be seen and understood in more intense later levels, each is still bounded by such layers of consciousness as he is able to inhabit and endure. We are still our own prisoners. So on earth also. In the spheres, the outer self can and must gradually drop away, allowing the interior self to be more fully lived in; and part of this process can already take place on earth. The second self – which is indeed much more one's self than the outer daily carapace – can gradually become the dominant partner, and bring to earth the riches of consciousness it can reach up to, which it shares with and derives from companions beyond. In time by practical outgoing action on earth and by inward work on itself, part of the daily self earns the right to begin to become absorbed into the inner self – to provide a working instrument for it. It finds itself by losing itself. Then a practical contribution can be made to the bringing of deeper values to earth. This is the real purpose of discarnate communication, and the recipient plays an essential part because he is obliged to bring it about in himself.

The recipient's part, however, is much less than the total situation. More will be said of this later in discussing the role of the mentor.

CHAPTER FIVE

PSYCHICAL RESEARCH AND MEDIUMSHIP

PSYCHICAL RESEARCH is a general term for applying scientific methods of gathering and assessing material seemingly, or claimed to be, from extrasensory sources, whether from persons on earth or purporting to speak from a discarnate source. Parapsychology, for the purpose of this chapter, can be regarded as a department within psychical research occupying a narrower field; its working parameters are often those of statistical measurement. Repeatable results are considered a central necessity for acceptable parapsychological evidence.

In the eyes of mediums, parapsychologists are little concerned with what mediumship sets out to do best, and are instead a great deal concerned with collecting material of little or no significance to mediums. In the careful avoidance of subjective elements, the central field of mediumship becomes virtually eliminated. Most mediums, of course, have little interest in material which might eventually prove that its source is in other areas than the one which seems entirely natural to themselves.

Mainstream psychical research, more broadly based than parapsychology, has over its history collected a considerable amount both of spontaneous and of organised material. The strong point of psychical research lies in its meticulous and systematic record-keeping. Within this field, as Professor Ian

Stevenson has recently pointed out, excellent examinations of the many problems which arise have been discussed in the Society for Psychical Research Presidential addresses, some of which are as valuable now as when originally produced many years ago.

The world of psychical research has in recent years largely removed itself from the world of purported discarnate communication, and is not concerned at all with the area of spiritual teaching. It adopts well tried scientific principles of measuring appropriate to the world of scientific objective observation. What it finds there and endeavours to measure is often distant from the field of mediumistic and spiritual experience, which is indeed little capable of being measured in that way. One important issue is: how can research concern itself with spiritual issues, and yet remain scientific? The question probably seems ridiculous to a good many researchers.

The work of the English body, the S.P.R., is largely carried out by individual planning, and the Society never takes a corporate view. Since the subject contains within itself a number of separate observational standpoints by no means necessarily fully inter-related, the Society's stance is clearly a wise one.

Looking back at its history of over 100 years, the fact remains that there still is no serious working hypothesis which a large number of researchers can accept; one which can then be further explored and enlarged or deepened or if necessary dismissed.

In zoology, fauna are studied and observed at first hand, and as far as possible in their natural habitat. In general, psychical researchers today are reluctant to study mediumship in this direct and obvious way. Researchers tend to have a distrust of mediums, and this forms one reason for refusing the personal experience of sitting with a medium and discovering and assessing what a medium can and cannot produce. A few do allow much work by mediums as being fair and honest. Many, however, feel on safer grounds with laboratory work. To bring a medium into a laboratory and set her a task of the experimenter's design perhaps has a parallel with placing an animal into a zoo, or even into a circus: a little is gained but much more is lost. Some of the original pioneers of the S.P.R. recognised the value of direct qualitative work. Myers and Lodge and others allowed experience of this kind to play upon them, and in spite of disappointments and confusions, this helped them to form and develop a serious understanding of this part of the field. May this trend indeed develop further and statistics take a less prominent role. May Hamlet be restored to the cast.

The conflict between measurement and anecdote goes deep. Psychical researchers, when they do not refuse to study mediumistic material directly, are not at home with it, and mediums are bad in imparting whilst working in this atmosphere.

In the early days of the S.P.R. the difficulty which constantly arose when endeavouring to assess evidential material was that it could not eliminate the possibility that it could have been derived by telepathy from living persons. It complicates the problem that some material from purported discarnate communicators is undoubtedly likely to have been received by telepathy from the recipient. Further, there is no firm scientific acceptance of telepathy itself. Indeed Sir Alister Hardy, Emeritus Professor of Zoology in Oxford University and a Gifford lecturer went further in saying that we still know nothing of how it comes about. Telepathy has therefore remained extremely hard either to prove or dismiss. Until it is discovered at least partially how it works, scientifically speaking it does not as yet fully exist. It is rather like a man unable to speak, and carrying no documents of identification.

Following the death of a few of the S.P.R. pioneers, a new type of evidence arrived which appeared to be a careful and deliberate plan to demonstrate telepathy from a discarnate source. These communications have come to be known as the cross-correspondences. In essence they consist of fragmentary, seemingly meaningless, statements by more than one sensitive, sometimes in different countries, which are later found, when put together, to be both meaningful and to point to a common source. In one case the sensitives lived respectively in England, India and America. Some, though not all, of the sensitives were highly educated ladies living in a scholarly field. A few professional mediums were also involved. Some items of recondite scholarship were given, presumably chosen as unlikely to be known to any of the sensitives, but likely to be known both to the recipient and to the seeming communicator. It is thought that the posthumous F. W. H. Myers could have been the leading spirit in devising these experiments. They continued for a number of years and are a mixture of the simple, the ingenious, and the complex. In all, the cross-correspondence material fills several hundred pages, and is not easy to study. Together it is almost impossible to avoid the conclusion that careful planning was involved. Obviously researchers sought to discover if a living person fraudulently planned and produced the material, or some of it, even possibly including one of the learned ladies, but nothing of this sort was ever discovered. There is no evidence of a plot from some living mind, or of how it could have been set in motion from such a source.

The cross-correspondences remain amongst the best and many would say quite the best, because best recorded, evidence of the survival of persons who had recently died and had been known to the S.P.R. investigators. No one has successfully set it aside. Researchers, if they found themselves still living after bodily death, had very good reason indeed to try to demonstrate both their existence and their ability to communicate with those on earth.

The cross-correspondences through this evidence of design clearly strike a blow at the principal objection to seemingly evidential discarnate material, that it can all be explained by telepathy from a living person or persons.

The cross-correspondence messages came to an end, as experiments eventually must. That they have seemingly made little impact upon many subsequent researchers is probably due to the material being so closely interwoven with deeply felt subjectivity. Many researchers are likely to consider this deflates their value. The cross-correspondences too seem incapable of repetition at the will of a researcher.

Another and important factor is claimed to have been spoken of after her death by 'Mrs Willett', herself one of the sensitivies who had participated in the cross-correspondences. In communications received by Geraldine Cummins in *Swan on a Black Sea* the Mrs Willett figure (after giving a large number of correct facts of her own earth life) speaks thus of the cross-correspondences:

> The several communicators were scholars, with intellects married to imaginations that cherished an ideal image of scholarly perfection in the evidence. The investigators and the mediums had sufficient imagination to envisage the . . . objective of perfection. Thus deep called to deep in a unified desire.

Elsewhere 'Mrs Willett' says: 'For really impressive results maintained over a long period, a trio is needed – the third in the trio is the sitter'. How different this is to the uneasy truce which tends to prevail between researcher and sitter.

Against such a canon of perfection, there is no doubt that a researcher who brings his own preconceived design to impose on the mediumistic situation is sadly preventing any opportunity for the kind of unity which 'Mrs Willett' deemed to be essential. He may be pursuing an ideal of his own, but almost certainly it will be no more than an intellectual one. It is well to recognise that 'Mrs Willett's' words were spoken from the very heart of psychical research. Yet the material seems to have little influenced later parapsychological thinking.

No serious student wishes to put a genuine researcher into the dock, but there is a time when it can be said that he puts himself there. Dr Rhine's famous statistical laboratory experiments in the field of telepathy and clairvoyance extended over a number of years. His principal medium, Mrs Garrett, who worked with him for two years, was unusual in that she often doubted the validity of her own gifts. She had a mind of good analytic quality, and was herself a highly interested observer in her own work. She tells Dr Rhine of her observations in working for him with sets of five Zener cards, a very useful *statistical* tool, but in her opinion useless for obtaining telepathic or clairvoyant results.

> However many thousands of tests might be made with the technique followed by Dr Rhine and his assistants, with the students and myself, their conclusions never changed my personal conviction that I was simply guessing at the symbols on those ESP cards. Clairvoyance, as I understand it, from my many years of work, depends, for me at least, on the use of an active *radiation* or *emanation* from persons or object as a stimulus. I have spoken of an *energy stimulus* as being necessary in clairvoyance and telepathy. I had such a stimulus in my work at Duke, not from the ESP cards, but from the interest and enthusiasm of Dr Rhine towards the work we were doing . . .
>
> In order to produce good results in trance and in other forms of supernormal sensing, it is also, according to my experience, necessary to have such a stimulation.

She then adds:

> . . . no serious experiment or good work to further such research can take place, without an ardent desire on the part of the experimenters or workers to achieve positive

results. Affirmation, faith and desire, are the *energy stimulus* needed to produce results, in science as well as in art and life. I know that in making this statement I am speaking of a subject which has rarely been recognised as of serious importance in the development of psychic research. *But I am convinced that many an investigator has confused a negative attitude with objectivity, and has thereby closed the doors on the necessary energy stimulus needed by the sensitive.*

It would seem that Dr Rhine, unfortunately, was unable to accept her account of her experience. The gathering of years of statistical experiments and the emergence of results slightly above chance were more important to him. It was hardly possible for him to allow her experience alone to nullify his work, as, if accepted, it would have done. Here scientific design and mediumistic experience were left to remain unresolved. An important opportunity may have been missed by Dr Rhine. It remains a good example of how difficult it is to bring psychical research and psychic sensitivity together in harmony.

Dr Rhine worked largely with university students. Though statistical purpose is legitimate and serious, is it unreasonable to consider it unlikely to be fruitful to study mediumship largely in those who do not possess it?

Whilst it is true that today there is rather more friendly sympathy towards professional mediums than formerly, it is still a fact that many psychical researchers choose not to obtain direct material of their own from mediums on the grounds that being largely subjective it would both fall outside the research parameters chosen, and from a scientific viewpoint would make invalid the researchers' own assessments.

Since few in fact take part in individual séances, the majority of researchers thus remain unskilled in this receptive field. Some there are who have obtained evidence; they then face the predicament that as researchers it is intellectually correct to say that what they have received gives no conclusive proof of survival, yet as individuals they come to accept privately that their own evidence has produced in them a personal conviction, or near conviction, or survival. A contradiction then arises within their own being. The researcher says 'No', whilst the private man in him says 'Yes'. Thus there is a conflict of integrities. This creates a predicament for honourable psychical researchers for whom separate values are telling these two separate things. This difficult situation is well recognised, although not so frequently spoken of publicly. The best way of resolving the contradiction surely lies in writing openly about it; not to suppress it, but to draw attention to it, so that educated debate upon the predicament can come about within psychical research itself. Unfortunately, however, open expression of this particular problem is perhaps feared by some lest it impedes an academic career, or arouses derision among peers who have not studied one iota of the subject.

It is important therefore for some who are not scientific researchers to take up a separate though complementary viewpoint, the other but equally necessary side of the coin, subjectively rooted and sometimes deeply so.

These two integrities need to be preserved, and if they cannot yet be combined, then separately until they can be. It is hard to see why qualitative work, however deeply subjective, cannot be allowed to produce a hypothesis based, like so much in science, on a probability basis, and, also like many scientific hypotheses to be discarded later if found unsound.

Speaking of the proper use of Occam's Razor, Sir Alister Hardy writes in *The Divine Flame*.

> This excellent principle, that of economy of thought, is certainly a valuable guide in general procedure but not if it makes us miss the truth in straining after an entirely false over-simplification.

In psychical research the use of Occam's Razor, the prin ciple of parsimony, clearly results at times in dismissing valuable material. In this speculative area it can pay to take a look at what exists beyond the minimum hypothesis. After all, there will always be cautious people ready to apply Occam's Razor. There is room for those who prefer to look at the complexity and possible riches in the material, which are likely through Occam to be obscured or ruled out. Other events exist in the psychical field as well as those looked for within parameters brought to it from elsewhere. The area of such field studies needs to be a very important part of psychical research. Here it is true we cannot look yet for certainty in what is observed; in explanation, it will always be possible, as long as we do not know the boundaries of the human mind (and we are never likely to know them all) to propound theories which often cannot be proved or dismissed. Most of the material is spontaneous, and it is doubtful whether more than a minimal part can come about in the laboratory. This is not decrying the laboratory of course, merely saying that much material can best be received and studied outside it.

The subject then needs some people who are not afraid to leave Occam's Razor on one side at times. However what sort of reality tests can then be applied to field material? If discarnate communication exists, it is after all basically an act of human relationship. In using survival as a working hypothesis, there comes a time when we must pass beyond what a posthumous Myers figure has called 'wearisomely presenting his credentials over and over again', and pass on to ask: can the posthumous Myers figure be a still living person, though discarnate, presenting his own fresh experience? To some an important evidential test has come to be this: can a communicator be convincingly seen to change and grow since his death? Does the late 'Mrs Willett' become indeed, a later 'Mrs Willett'? Did the T. E. Lawrence figure, as *Post-Mortem Journal* states, somewhat painfully overcome his former sense of his own superiority to other beings? Did he also overcome what in the script he calls 'twisted emotions' which he had on earth? Mediumistic material is nearer to the field of art than that of science. We are dealing with reports of emotional changes, changes in character; we are in the field of value judgments and of assessing the worth of the witness. Value judgments are concerned with much of the real stuff of living before death. Must it be so different after death? We are in an area where validity takes on another quality than amenity to measurement.

Change and growth are interesting and valuable as told by communicators reporting back in the early stages. Later when a more stable situation has been reached change and growth are still very present. Those who persevere with communication are likely to be confronted, as we shall see in a later chapter, with a discarnate teacher at a level of insight which is clearly superior to that of the sensitive's own normal level. Are we to be content with the economical concept that material introduced in the trance state arrived at by dissociation on the medium's part, sometimes produces a side of herself which is demonstrably wiser than the medium's conscious self? Does the part become more than the whole? Or is a discarnate mind truly, if imperfectly, sometimes producing much of the material? If a communicator, apart from trance, says an enhancement of consciousness has come about for him since death, and demonstrates it in his words, what else than a value judgment can one make? How else evaluate a mind seemingly become enlarged by subsequent experience, even if described in a way sometimes misaligned or otherwise limited by its passage through the mind of the medium? We are dealing with a double difficulty in this necessarily imperfect situation. There is plenty of room here for subjective confusion. Experience shows it can be as dangerously facile to attribute the whole of the material to that discarnate mind as to attribute the whole of it to the medium. In this part of the research field, researchers naturally prefer their own orderly approach than to struggle with the anecdotal shapelessness of other witnesses. Hence in general they fight shy of this part of the field.

In subjective experience a balance cannot be struck by any one individual, though there can be powerful opinions and beliefs based on vivid material. Better when a corpus grows up of parallel material gathered and assessed by a considerable number of recipients of careful approach and of many different temperaments, who do not hesitate for social or professional reasons to make their allegiances known. If it is said that once you enter the field of value judgments this is no longer psychical research, such a view cannot be quarrelled with. Nevertheless, value judgments and all that clusters around them are a highly important part of human nature, and if we survive it is surely reasonable to suppose that they are likely to continue to be a highly important part of discarnate living also, and therefore worthy of being studied at some length.

Eileen Garrett once promoted a three-day conference in London which concerned itself a good deal with the problem of how to get fresh material which might throw conclusive light upon the survival problem. It seemed to be the balance of opinion among the eminent psychical researchers present that something of a deadlock had been reached. Since then serious attention has been given to near-death and out-of-body experiences, however subjective. They may in time also throw light upon the mind/brain controversy. Cannot suggestive field material be used by more psychical researchers to ponder upon; urging them to speak at times in Wittgenstein style, *as if* we survive and *as if* would-be communicators are present or partly present somewhere behind all the tiresome occasional hazes and confusions and difficulties of third party mediumship, and to set up, without commitment, a working hypothesis accordingly?

INNER EYE, LISTENING EAR

In the last hundred years, psychology has worked within a field rich in subjective experience. Psychology has crept towards being granted scientific acceptance because it has demonstrably achieved therapeutic results in a number of disturbed persons where it has been able to distinguish chains of cause and effect in the behaviour of the psyche, in patterns undoubtedly repeated in many persons. Nevertheless, human beings of course vary greatly, but when they seem to act in similar ways and repeat already observed patterns, we gradually give some credence to a highly trained and honest professional researcher. If we see that some psychiatrists come to observe independently much the same things, though they may well apply different concepts from one another, we are ready to accept that a reality situation exists, that patients do have similar problems, that psychiatrists do discover them, and in some cases effect cures.

As against this, in psychical research professional scepticism towards the material is more pronounced and longer continuing. When a good many descriptions, claiming to report discarnate adventures, speak of rather similar experiences, it is easier merely to say, because of the generally suspect nature of the material, 'Our source for all this is in mediums, and one sensitive is likely to repeat what another has formerly written or said, and therefore is probably not producing any really new material'. A tendency grows to give little value to the element of mutual support and to pay little interest in either obvious or subtle differences between one account and another. Similarly when discarnate beings in their accounts change and grow within themselves, it is open to us to say that this too can be put down to fantasy of the medium and is no real proof that there are discarnate persons who can do anything of the sort. Alternatively one can move into the qualitive field and be willing to judge discarnate material as one would that of living human beings. Human sensibility is a natural organic thing. The super-ESP theory to explain evidence relating to one discarnate person sets it up as an amalgam of telepathic perceptions drawn from several living persons, none of whom the sensitive knows or has known, in some way that nobody, including the sensitive, can explain. Nor as far as I know has any researcher attempted to bring about similar results experimentally. The super-ESP theory has thus come to look more and more like defensive armchair theorising.

It becomes important to decide, when the paper evidence comes together and points in a unifying way to a particular human being, whether these evidential straws in the wind make up more than a man of straw. It is then that one faces giving up a seat on the fence.

Different difficulties arise in multiple evidence, when a communicator is claimed to speak through more than one sensitive.

Surely it is not too absurd to conceive that a communicator can find it impossible to convey significant information through the mind of one sensitive but is able to do so through the help of another one. However, the same communicator, claiming to appear through a second medium can deny all knowledge of what was said to the same recipient through the first medium, or even denies he has appeared at all. Whilst this in an undoubtedly disturbing situation one cannot wholly deny the right of a communicator to attempt to correct himself. It is not easy to decide who is really speaking the words: the original communicator in some difficulty, or simply the second medium. If a number of instances of this kind of difficulty are seen to come about, and are reported accurately, there is at least a chance that after a while we may detect patterns which throw light upon the whole difficult process of communication. It is easy to write things off too hastily. What does seem sure is that a purported communicator sometimes only has a slender hold on the medium's mind, and there can then be confusion and misunderstanding. In such cases, some recipients prefer to write off such a communicator entirely and leave the underlying situation as hard to assess as ever.

Here perhaps is the place to give a picture of how a sensitive and a psychical researcher tend to regard one another in a standard mediumistic session. Unfortunately, if there is a fundamental lack of sympathy, an unworthy picture can result on both sides. Some researchers look on mediumship as a low-class operation, not sanitised enough to be worthy of a scientist's professional enquiry. He looks, perhaps, on the sensitive as liable to be fraudulent or an insecure witness, or of poor mental calibre. This attitude is basically made up of two kinds of suspicion. A fundamental suspicion of the reality of a medium's gift leads to suspicion of her honesty. Most researchers know that it is necessary to win the medium's confidence, and they presume that clumsy masculine fair words are enough, but the medium seldom judges by this. She is more responsive to underlying feelings than to words. There is a big difference between careful verbal reticence and inner mental stone-walling, and a sensitive is likely to be very aware of the latter.

How does the sensitive in turn see the researcher? Usually as a highly intelligent man whom she nevertheless looks on as being in the kindergarten class in the psychical field. She sometimes regards him as wasting her time. The comment mediums make on psychical researchers, even sympathetic ones, is nearly always the same: 'What a pity he does not study mediumship more closely'. She doesn't mind initial scepticism. She does mind a resolute refusal to move away from it or to learn the *ABC* of receiving communications. Thus it is not easy for either sensitive or researcher to do justice to the other. Mediumship is uncertain in its results and seldom precise in the way researchers require. Mediums, defensive in a socially unacceptable profession, frequently compensate by being both over-sure and over-emphatic.

A sensitive's mind is essentially free-ranging, and that is different from wide-ranging. She is so plastic and receptive that when working at less than her best it is difficult for her not to skip from one theme to another, and from one communicator to another. It requires a much deeper degree of concentration to pass beyond this; a level which is at once relaxed and yet steadily focussed. Like other disciplines it is only won by practice. A medium usually hates not being able to play everything by ear, and dislikes having to follow someone else's set procedure. That is one reason why she is usually so inadequate when taking part in research experiments. If questions are asked of her outside her own competence, she is likely to produce wild answers, often unrelated to the real context of what is asked. At the best of times her delicate impressions are liable to be misinterpreted by the listener and sometimes by herself. The recipient tends to think them more clear-cut and factual than they are. They often arrive as we have seen in a fragmentary way with little shape, and it is then far from easy for a medium to express them in a way which will satisfy a researcher.

The extra sensory faculty tends too to retreat and refuse to work for unsympathetic clients, and on some occasions reluctantly for those who have no emotional need. Deep emotion in a communicator and recipient can lead to strong evidence. A medium's own compassion arouses and intensifies her perceptions. Some psychical researchers can readily think when the sensitive does badly for them that this is really her normal form, and that they themselves are detached enough to see it in an unclouded and realistic way, and that people who claim to have had much better results than theirs are likely to have grasped readily at emotional threads, or in various ways misled themselves. But for such other persons the material may really have been much better, not merely misreported by credulous listeners. A good deal of the responsibility for a poor session rests upon the recipient, whether a researcher or a person in deep emotional need.

Not many psychical researchers will be willing to relate to this approach. They have their own different problems to overcome. The researcher expects to have full control and direction of the experimental design. He often decides what he is going to call upon his subject to attempt. In everyday professional mediumistic performance the sensitive, as we have seen, needs to be left a free choice to produce the material which comes to her in her own way. The result then has its own full immediacy, and can provide what to careful recipients becomes gradually accepted as largely correct and spontaneous evidence strongly suggestive of an active discarnate mind and heart.

The canons applied by a psychical researcher are very different, both mentally and emotionally, from the needs of a deeply bereaved person, and these again are different from those who are seeking for a spiritual life pattern which will serve them well on earth, and hopefully in an after life also. Some are interested too in descriptive help from those who show evidence of having altered and deepened their being as a result of work-tasks and experience they now record. The better mediums are able to contact communicators who offer a helpful hand to those now facing various problems of their own on earth. They offer a companionship of spirit to those willing to work with what they are able to impart.

It is not realistic to make an assumption that all observation and experience of mediumship outside the attention of psychical research is trivial, and to condemn the profession of mediumship itself similarly, nor on the other hand is it realistic to complain that all researchers condemn everything.

Some members of the Society for Psychical Research are now coming to the opinion that statistical parapsychology has for too long taken up something of a cuckoo's role in the nest of psychical research, and has indeed forced out of the nest the qualitative evidence not to be found in statistics. Clearly serious research is to be respected when its results are negative, since these can therein point to significant clues not found elsewhere. The same respect, however, can hardly be given to the occasional risible theory which gains the honour of appearing in the Journal or even in Proceedings of the S.P.R. There has been a researcher's theory that when D. D. Home, whilst in trance and well-observed, floated horizontally out of one window and back through another, it was produced by the help of conspirators on the roof, who enabled him to abseil over space. Not one iota of evidence of the existence of conspirators was produced, and one rather wonders how they would have surmounted the problem of getting Home out of the room when under close and multiple observation.

Then there is the theory that mediumistic phenomena come about through the presence of underground water. Do mediums congregate only where underground water abounds, whether or not it is known to be there? And how does the presence of water help to produce the evidence for the medium to relay, and the emotions which inform it?

Another theory from a more serious researcher endeavoured to show that psychometric information is produced as a result of sweat on the owner's fingers whilst handling the psychometric object. How do sweat particles sometimes convey psychometric information relating to a former owner of the object, perhaps many years before?

It is not enough to show that most anecdotal evidence can be written off by inventing alternative explanations, unless, as Dr Thouless has said, the explanation is examined as rigorously as the original material. All too often it is not closely examined at all.

It is legitimate to say then that enquiry into the paranormal has fallen into two separate halves, that of scientific research and that of direct experiential search, which have largely and unhealthily remained too far separated from each other. Psychical research uses statistical methods and repeatability requirements more appropriate to measurement in entirely different fields. Direct experience is related mainly to subjective assessment, sometimes based only on partially and poorly kept records. Each is observing a different part of the field, with different methods of observation. Each is inadequate to the observational needs of the other.

A good step towards integrating these two diverse groups of material is for a much more direct study to be made on the scientific side into the nature of mediumship and the experience of mediums, and how this relates to the more intuitive factors displayed at times in other human activities, including telepathic faculties at work in scientific speculation. On the experiential and subjective sides, there is little to prevent the gradual development of closer attention to understanding such human qualities as will lead to a closer and deeper command of the telepathic faculty.

Above all, the establishing and developing of a working hypothesis, whether or not subsequently discarded, might well prove to be the main road so long looked for in psychical research.

CHAPTER SIX

THE COMMUNICATOR

1

IF THE TELEPHONE BELL rings, naturally the caller is expected to identify himself. In post-mortem communication, necessitating something far more complex than a telephone, it is not enough to seek the speaker's identity. One needs to estimate also as far as is possible his present status and stature. This involves a number of factors, overlapping and hard to keep separate, each bringing its own kind of difficulty. Four such factors can readily be named.

The first factor concerns the communicator. How much does a communicator know? Does he himself always know how much he knows, and how can we know how far he is right? A post-mortem F. W. H. Myers points out – I say *a* post-mortem Myers, and not *the* post-mortem Myers – that a newly dead person knows as little of the real nature of the world now around him as an infant does of life on earth; the difference of course is that on death he has his adult thoughts and feelings to help him find out. The evidence clearly shows it to be a myth that on death all is shown, that death is the great revealer. So in asking how much a communicator can be expected to know, one has to decide whether he is a tenderfoot; or a senior, perhaps even ancient, though not decayed thereby. On the contrary he could have gained a much expanded consciousness as a result of his longer experiences. Indeed, part of his consciousness and experience can be expected to lie beyond our present ken, and so be only partly communicable to us: we are not able to share it all. The remaining three factors all involve difficulties and obstructions in finding out this status of the communicator.

The second factor is this: whatever he knows, how much of it can a communicator impart? As we have seen he can be unable to transmit it accurately because hampered by difficulties in the process of communication itself.

Allied, but again to be distinguished from it, is the third factor: how much of what the communicator means to say becomes distorted by the sensitive, who is after all a limited human instrument in whom distortion can come about unconsciously but also semi-consciously. The medium too is sometimes unable to go all the way with the communicator.

The fourth factor – one overlooked more often than it should be – is that much of what is said can be misunderstood or otherwise altered by the recipient himself.

Taking these four factors in the reverse order, we have (1) misunderstanding by the recipient; (2) distortion by the sensitive; (3) the hampering process of communication as experienced by the communicator; and (4) our real quest: the communicator's status and stature.

2

Factor one – misunderstanding by the recipient. Not to put too fine a point upon it, how far can that which is imperfect on his side of this relationship adversely influence the situation? He will assess his communicator both by the evidence, and by the value-judgments implied in what is said. But suppose the recipient resists these value-judgments stubbornly, because they conflict with those of his own he desires to continue to hold. They are probably much more comfortable to hold. How far is he able to be disinterested, how far does he indeed welcome the truth of the situation? Is he passionately enough concerned about it? He may not want the truth; he may go further and try to force it into his own direction. He can seek self-justification instead of being willing to change his views.

It is not easy to be ready within oneself to find out what the communicator really is attempting to say, as near to 100% as any imperfect human being can get. Unfortunately too the communicator's meaning, as reported, may well be not too clear. There may be some confusion about areas of reference; but if so it is of course no good just preferring to believe it must refer to the area one wants it to.

Another challenge arises when the communicator focusses on a blind spot in his listener. It is hard to estimate oneself correctly, as even so deep a soul as the nun Frances Banks found.

> A true humbling ... to find that you did so little when you would have done so much; that you went wrong so often when you were sure that you were right.

The communicator must be able to touch on whatever area he wishes if there is to be the basis for a good communication; the listener too needs to endeavour to bring his real self to the encounter. The benefit of the situation is that in some cases the communicator has moved on further than the recipient and because of this finds it easier to be himself. This is an early way of recognising his status.

It is an advantage, too, that the recipient no longer needs to keep face with his communicator in quite the same way as with someone on earth. A very real imaginative participation is needed sometimes to find the true meaning behind perhaps very imperfect words; here unfortunately a good many psychical researchers turn away because it is an area, important though it is, in which they lack interest, since it contains much subjective content.

3

The second factor concerns possible distortions by the medium, working either consciously or in trance. The process of reaching the inner attunement which is required of a sensitive can be very exacting; in the case of some the preparation can begin two or three hours before a trance. Preparation is often insufficiently performed. Mrs Gladys Osborne Leonard once recognised to her horror that some words spoken in trance and then reported to her had been read by herself that same morning in her daily paper; from that time on, she would never read a newspaper before working. Unfortunately this sort of self-discipline is rare.

At times the communicator loses hold, and the flow of the thoughts and feelings of the medium partially take over instead, though still in the guise of the communicator. Here the recipient should not begin to argue. It is better to listen quietly and wait for the communicator to take firm hold again, as he will probably do a few minutes later.

The larger the stature of a teacher-communicator, the greater the degree of renunciation called for from the sensitive. The time factor too enters in here, a long period, possibly as much as twenty years apparently being sometimes needed fully to attune the sensitive to the deeper rhythms of the teacher's perceptions, or to overcome firmly-rooted emotional antipathies, such as to reincarnation. To some it points to the existence of a mind at work independently of the medium to find, over a term of years, a sensitive in her everyday self stoutly denying reincarnation, whilst her trance control goes on teaching it. Usually in the end the trance control prevails, and he would then be likely to be better able to go on to express further aspects, which have been fully present all through those years in his mind, but hitherto incommunicable. Fortunately, the plasticity of a sensitive's mind – just how much one finds out when dealing with them in everyday situations – is a help to them in overcoming their resistances. Later on, the opposite difficulty can be seen gradually to arise; the teacher's philosophy having been accepted and passed through the sensitive's mind so often, she gradually takes on those ideas as her own, both through reading the transcripts of her addresses and through the very transit of the material through her mind when originally given, even if in deep trance. The careful listener recognises that some material is basically, though not literally, repetitive; and that on such a day no new ideas are likely to flow.

It becomes apparent over many years in watching many sensitives, that they are of lesser stature than their teachers mentally, emotionally and spiritually; this too brings about a conviction that there are indeed independent beings at work. Jungian concepts require that these teachers are looked on either as a split-off part of the self, or as representing part of the collective unconscious, as in the archetypal figure of the old wise man. But we still know so little of the constitution of man as a spiritual being. It is difficult for instance to regard the very circumstantially evidential 'Mrs Willett' in *Swan on a Black Sea* either as a split-off of the medium, Geraldine Cummins, or as an archetypal figure.

4

Each of the four factors becomes harder to assess as we move closer into the discarnate area. The third factor relates to the hampering process of communication. 'Mrs Willett' describes how in recalling a former earth-memory, say of herself as a young girl, she does not merely remember her, she *becomes* her again for the moment, she re-assumes her. We do not altogether know what limitations of memory accompany these temporary repossessions. Can the re-assumed young girl at that moment recapture qualities won only at a later part of her life, if asked to express them instantaneously? It seems unlikely, nor is it reasonable to expect it. One cannot be dogmatic here, but it is an interesting possible aspect of some failures of evidence.

To give an example of a more common type of misunderstanding. It often looks as if the communicator has to learn up his part beforehand, so to speak, and then do his best with the selection of facts he has brought with him. Here the sceptic smiles, but his smile does not harm those who are trying to find out the facts from experience. This certainly suggests that during the interview the communicator's full memory is not accessible to him. Communicators interested in the mediumistic process have spoken of this predicament, including such a well-known researcher as Sir William Barrett, F.R.S., a founder member of the S.P.R. When speaking to his wife after his death, he says he is at this moment less than the being he will resume after the session is over. Perhaps it is not unlike when the eyepieces of the binocular are focussed on a foreground detail and as a consequence omit some of the wider landscape around.

What, it must be asked, makes a good communicator? Naturally the desired recipient is also involved, since a similarity or harmony of temperament, sometimes perhaps made up of opposite qualities, is likely to ease some of the difficulties. In general, it is probably true that an extroverted communicator is likely to do better than an introvert, at least in terms of exchange. It also depends on the subjects on the agenda, and the depth of communication hoped for, and here the introvert may do better than the extrovert.

Communicators say that the process is essentially very simple, but of considerable difficulty to execute satisfactorily.

THE COMMUNICATOR

Without doubt there is required a completeness of concentration which many find they are unable to hold for long. The thread can come to an end before intended, there will be an apparent abrupt breaking off.

This is one reason why some communicators become disappointed and give up any further attempts. Successful communication requires a firmly held purpose, mental and emotional alike. Some say they like to learn by watching a more experienced communicator at work. It also needs to be recognised that, as F.W.H. Myers has said, a communicator does not necessarily have to be present at a séance. He projects a thought form of himself, which has a limited degree of animation. Perhaps this has some resemblances to sending a cassette through the post. Certainly it could account for why some communicators appear unable to deal with questions, especially when introducing a changed subject, even if it is expected that he would be able to deal with the question easily enough if his whole attention and memory were present.

It is difficult to come to understand what processes can be involved, but easier to recognise difficulties likely to be present, any one of which can break the threads between the three persons involved. Sometimes it is obviously very difficult for a communicator to draw the medium's full attention, especially in a subject in which she is not versed. Here one sees one reason why the medium, when listening telepathically, needs to be undisturbed by her sitter.

This is a difficult part of the subject to study, since we often have to accept statements in a way which cannot be properly checked. We can do little more than compare the statements about the process involved with the successes and faults and failures which our own experience observes, the more so since the medium's attention at the time has to be very fully occupied with the person she is contacting, and she is not free to range around other points of observation. In other words, the finer the level of the recipient's attention, and the underlying qualities which bring it about the better can be the emerging understanding of what is going on behind the scenes, and of the varying spiritual levels which bring about and colour the words employed. As in deep and important dialogues on earth, the more complete the participation which each brings to it, the more easily the real and sometimes difficult issues will emerge. This is about as far different as can be from when a recipient is content with just sitting comfortably and waiting for the medium to give good news without intending to make any effort to respond seriously.

The communicator then, it is clear, has a number of difficulties to meet and overcome. There is the group of these which cluster around the transmission process, and the communicator's ability to overcome the problems of intention and concentration. Others cluster around poor attention and poorer motives in the recipient which lowers or damages the occasions. Others lie at the door of the mediums for whom other matters are allowed to be more important than the message she is or could be imparting. Goodwill, good spirits, good motivation and perseverance gradually do much to raise communication nearer to what is intended at its source.

All of us feel disillusioned at times by the incompleteness of communication, but then we see so little of the difficulties. This is why more refined communicators contrast communication with communion, and ask us to pass over to the latter, when discarnate soul can speak to earth soul in meditation, or in an extra-sensory and private way. Here it is pointless to expect the minutiae of evidence – ('Did your grandmother sleep on her right side?'). Conviction comes far more through the quality of the communion. What is the essential contrast between communication and communion? In communication the communicator is at something of a disadvantage in having to speak mainly to the everyday self of the recipient. In communion, one tries to leave that self a little behind, to raise one's level of consciousness and be in touch with the part of one's inner self which comes nearer to sharing some common ground with the communicator's whole present self; soul to soul, more than personality to personality. So in communion the telepathic process is more at home as it were, its impressions can be shapely and direct, if the recipient can find the stillness to capture them.

5

The fourth and last factor, and our real quest; the communicator's true stature when unhampered by the local difficulties of communicating. We cannot hope for a perfect picture of him. Take the simple distinction already made between the recently dead, still largely encumbered within the net of their earth memories, desires and beliefs; intermediate ones, able to stand back and speak more objectively of what they have found; and seniors free or comparatively free from compulsions, able to speak with compassion and dispassion.

If early communicators are living to a certain extent among their own illusions, then they will largely communicate illusion. Part of what they see around them is a representation – which seems objective to them – of aspects of their own nature and such areas are likely to be shared with others of similar spiritual level. In these representational scenes, one would expect an element of assistance from knowledgeable beings, acting both as stage-manager and teacher in this act of psycho-drama. One intelligent man tells of his astonishment after death at finding how literal some newcomers can be. He sees a woman carrying around two large suitcases. She comes to a narrow, arched door with 'Entrance to the Kingdom of Heaven' inscribed above it. As she is French, the words are written in French. She won't put the suitcases down because she says they contain records of all her good deeds. In considerable distress she finds that as long as she holds on to the suitcases she can't get through the narrow door. It is hard to think of a neater picture to show her the real motive behind her good deeds. Quite obviously the scene is not objective; but it does serve an objective teaching purpose.

If a man has not found his own psychological centre, or has not made a full enough inner psychological journey while on earth, he will face the need in some form to do it there.

If one accepts that practical activities can be carried on in the inner world, book-binding for instance, one is probably both right and wrong. A mental environment can be created capable of being shared with other people, which while being illusory also represents an immediate need of the soul. Bound books created thus are unlikely to outlast the need of the craftsman who produced them.

Any advice given from these early levels will be little wiser than could have been given on earth. It may or may not be good; it will certainly be limited in its insight. After death men learn through being willing to change themselves even if the process is a painful one. Oliver Lodge found after death that his ready capacity to go on learning which he had possessed on earth still stood him now in very good stead. Indeed, lack of willingness seems a great obstacle, and can lead to a degree of encapsulation. Conan Doyle had some unpleasant things to swallow when he found a number of his former strongly held Spiritualistic concepts had been wrong. In studying communicators at work he found some were impersonators, and this gave him considerable disquiet. Looking at Spiritualists from his point of vantage he found them altogether too complacent. He himself was too big to refuse to accept what he now saw.

The purpose of many communications is to encourage us to acclimatise ourselves to these after-death states, by starting to clothe ourselves now with new attributes. This is what Oliver Lodge meant in advising people to learn to live in their

THE COMMUNICATOR

spirit body now, saying that many men on earth are only alive in about 10% of their true self. People often say with some complacency: 'Well, I shall be quite content to learn about the spirit world when I get there'. But communicators like Lodge want to help us to make use of the unlived 90% part of ourselves right away, for our present as well as future benefit.

This process of help is continued by communicators of senior status. This is where the value and the fascination of these investigations really lie, though obviously the vital preliminary is first to feel assured of survival. Such an assurance in turn, brings a conviction that life is worth living now and still more worth living hereafter, and that this worth is likely to be expressed in a growth of consciousness individual and shared. Seniors, if we can contact them or they us, demonstrate something of what this growth brings. Of course, like many other promises, there is a resulting condition: whatever helping hand is given is of little avail unless the listener then becomes willing to perform his part of the work upon himself.

In order to get to the core of this problem of status, it is necessary to recognise that all external factual tests, which are really designed to discover any mediumistic error or intervention, are irrelevant to the deeper levels of communication, though they form of course a salutary discipline of investigation. If a mediumistic control says he was an ancient Egyptian and shows, for instance, that he knows when horses were first introduced into Egypt, it may establish one's confidence, or one may prefer to go to the trouble to show the medium could have come about the information in some other and normal way, but it is nothing to do with any spiritual relationship. The only way to find value in such a relationship which might be called a vertical one, is to experience it and then to cultivate its fruits. As already said its value is not confined to what comes through the medium's help. There is no need to be dependent only on the medium. That is, or ought to be, only the tip of the iceberg. This is where communion comes in. It continues to be available to deep private inner listening, other than in the mediumistic interview, but a communicator is still likely to be sometimes involved in initiating the themes and images which arise privately.

The critic reads the words of discarnate teachers, and usually mutters 'platitudes', but in doing so he turns away from his own inner self which the words are intended to arouse, and to which they are a way-shower. Due to inadequacies in the mediumistic performance, the phrases can be occasionally painful to those blessed with a sense of words, but nevertheless they often point the way to an experience which the listener can then reach. Ordinary everyday communicators, new arrivals, speak of times of solitary quiet, where further processes of assimilation come to them. Vertical relationships are largely concerned with a similar awakening of an inner self on earth, and the bringing to it a readiness for spiritual growth.

CHAPTER SEVEN

THE MEDIUM AT WORK: INNER LEVELS

IT IS NOW TIME to consider a further, more intimate, part of the medium's task, that of speaking to the more interior side of her client; and the need to make a considerably closer link with her communicator.

It can readily be seen that to provide initial factual evidence really only needs two or three distinct and decisive facts. The client very often lets the medium down by going on demanding more and more earthly facts. Both medium and client, however, are later called upon to become attuned to receive material which is decisive in quite a different way, which plays upon the inner self of the client, and awakens or re-awakens depths long forgotten or never yet touched. This is not likely to come about if the client allows his daily self to be too intrusive, instead of awaiting new things the communicator may have come to convey.

The medium has to endure old obstinacies in her client, and endeavour to bring about a fresh alignment in him. But she does not wish her encounter to turn into a battlefield.

For significant work to come about the medium is therefore confronted with the task either of constantly adjusting her attention to meet her client, or else of endeavouring to preserve her own best level, without too much regard to her client and his present and often ignorant pursuit of aims which will do much to destroy the texture of what she is trying to produce. Mediums differ from one another in a number of ways; in the choice of where she can best place her attention; in her natural sensitivities towards one area rather than another; in her ability to overcome areas of superficial habit which would otherwise build up in her practice; in her balance of attention between client and communicator; in her judgment of what priority is best to choose between her client's involuntary insensitivity and her communicator's urgency. She also is aware when her communicator, or her recipient, or both, are unfamiliar with the intricacies of the process. An unambitious medium, of course, can avoid or lessen some of these difficulties by nearly always confining her attention to very simple everyday levels, and leave to others the depths which she is unable to meet and deal with.

As in many caring professions obstacles of character alike in herself and her clients conspire together to reduce the quality of the interview. The sunlight within her becomes overcast, nor can she be expected to overcome all the human frailties which limit or spoil so much in earth relationships. Add to this that the best field in which the medium works is an inner one, tenuous, delicate, hidden, and below the surface, it is not surprising how she often falls short and how often too, when the medium is on target the recipient in turn fails to apprehend the subtleties involved and erroneously translates much into familiar levels where it does not belong.

In time a medium recognises that she is also a member of a team, of which she is only the outermost member. Good communicators bring good order. An early question for the medium lies in the establishing of order within herself too. Certainly there is more than one level available from which she can receive and it can be said that every level requires its own discipline and its accompanying training.

Thus mentors sometimes show that they have an exact and intimate knowledge of their pupil's spiritual and material situation. Such teachers, without being prophetic or precognitive, sometimes pass comments based on seeing more deeply than the pupil can for himself. Douglas Johnson's guide, Chiang, for instance, several times made comments concerning myself and my working colleagues which I did not accept at the time, but later experience showed him to have been entirely correct. Ronald Fraser, the novelist, told how Mrs Grace Cooke's mentor spoke a few words to him which showed such exact knowledge of his previous six months work that the mentor might have been looking over his shoulder every morning as he wrote. This novelist, an acute and critical observer, was certain the comments were not derived from his own mind, although he was well aware of the possibility.

If the medium will not disturb her own everyday level the communicator's message in turn becomes reduced and the inner world he speaks of takes on in her words too much resemblance to the earth world. At this level little that is new is learned.

As the medium wills to deepen her work she can begin to discover a new largeness of faculty. It tells her things to pass on to her recipients which she herself often does not fully understand. It calls for a belief in her communicator's knowledge as surpassing her own. This entails a period of gradually becoming able to sense for herself the validity or otherwise of her new material. Then she is no longer an impoverished medium living on the shores of gobbledegook, or giving teachings which she does not always know she is misunderstanding. 'Beware of nebulous glorification' is the excellent advice of one mentor whose own words are much deeper than their apparent simplicity.

In true communication, not of a surface kind, what the medium receives is often a stealing in of telepathic impressions of an extremely delicate kind, arriving when she is at peace with her feelings, and which are both received and given in harmony. These telepathic impressions come more clearly as communication deepens, in a way which is sometimes wordless, though clear and direct in impact. It is more like a *knowing*. If the medium then finds words arising in her mind these are likely to reflect the 'message' closely, but at times when communicator and medium are in less than full contact, the medium may be obliged to speak no more than the gist, sometimes a clumsy gist, of what is intended.

Communicators, especially intellectuals, are sometimes unable to bring about in themselves the necessary patience of attention. One such, a former prominent member of the S.P.R., complained after her death of communication processes as haphazard, and one sympathises with this researcher finding her accustomed razor sharpness of mind apparently not able to reproduce itself through her message. There was also, it should be said, a lack in this communicator, who was somewhat at war with herself about even attempting the task. Towards the end, she said, 'You see, it is hopeless'. But she did give thanks to the continuing patience of the medium.

When a medium is prepared to accept the discipline of the deeper levels, part of her work will be to distinguish when her client has come, perhaps unconsciously, for an answer to a spiritual question. The client is often unlikely to be able to formulate the question rightly. He is only aware of some unidentified lack or need within him. That is a true sitter. Other clients seek to satisfy a need in an entirely wrong coin. The medium is ready with bread, but the lazy part of the client says: 'Give me a stone'. Estelle Roberts's guide Red Cloud, used to say: 'You do not always ask us the right questions but we try to give you the right answers'. He could perceive what the sitter needed to know, but was not fully aware of.

The inner aura is another name for the deeper part of one's being; it contains the record of a person's entire inner and outer experience, much more than he knows in his everyday self in the shifting territory of his outer aura. The inner aura is best not thought of in physical or quasi-physical terms but as an aspect of consciousness. Knowledge of an appointed life task, for instance, is embedded in the inner aura. A medium cannot always hope to share all of her own mentor's vision of it. What she is allowed to impart usually deals in a very practical way with the next spiritual step for the client.

This is not for the more rank and file mediums. They can well be effective in outer fields of evidence. They are needed for that. After all, some communicators are not ready to go deep, nor are some recipients. Their present need nevertheless has still to be met. It is the familiar matter of horses for courses. The one who is truly able to read into the inner aura will gradually attract appropriate clients because of her own spiritual qualities; compassion, perhaps, or love, or generosity, or discrimination, and almost certainly humility, with which her own life has enriched her and made her available for embarking on this deeper work. Other mediums have these or other soul qualities but choose to use them as yet in less deep waters.

There are indications that communicators who are spiritual mentors do a certain amount of 'reading' the inner aura. After all what is 'written' there is the most authentic possible record of the person's full nature; it is an area from which the mentor can be sure he can see where help is most needed.

An essential recognition for the client is that he is not in this life on probation to become a spiritual being, he is one already. The medium needs to know when it is wise to speak of reincarnation, of threads of continuity between the present man and his long term past; this thread is essentially a causal one. As Buddhists say, speaking of a man's essential nature, if you want to know what you have formerly been look at what you now are.

The inner aura is providing evidence of the client's past spiritual gains and losses. For practical purposes, of course, the medium is mostly concerned with helping the client to deal with the present. She is enabled to describe and advise upon what the client has insufficiently seen, or may not have seen at all. Naturally the client is the only one who can do the actual work of facing and curing his predicaments. That is why a good medium, like a good psychologist, does not tell the client what to do. She helps him to see for himself a picture of the symptoms in his character. He then comes to see what he needs to work upon in inward as well as outward ways. Hitherto he may have felt uncomfortable about his own situation without as yet caring to find out why, or he may know it more fully but deny in his daily life what it is telling him. The inner aura is a living, vibrating continuum, the workshop wherein the pupil's present is gradually wrought into his future. It is also played upon by forces from the inner world, both good and evil. Clearly for a medium to be allowed to read into the inner aura is something of a sacred task. All this forms a very rich quarry for mediumistic work, the opening of doors into a wider landscape of consciousness.

All training for mediumship, and for all spiritual healing too, can be condensed into one word: attunement. The task of reading the inner aura has both an active and a passive side. Where the medium has the inner stillness to listen in depth, and above all enough love and compassion of an impersonal kind, the inner aura of the sitter will begin to unfold itself directly to her view. It will tell only that part of its secrets which the medium needs to become aware of. It is usually concerned with the more permanent values partly hidden by the recipient's outer character; with the more deeply rooted parts of his make up. The outer client will sometimes be suffering very active thoughts and feelings, and be unable to relate them to these hidden parts of his being. They can stand up and hit him; perhaps he feels very aggrieved towards some person or towards his life pattern, or towards life itself. There is the common selfish cry: 'Why did this have to happen to me? What have I done to deserve it?'

At such times, though the real sources lie deeper, the client's agitated outer aura very much comes into the picture. It calls for instant help. Clearly it is not possible always to make complete distinctions between outer and inner aura. They play upon one another. The medium tries to see the factors in the inner aura which the client is over-expressing or else altogether denying in his outer aura. So the medium uses information in order to help bring about a better relationship between outer and inner aura. A medium needs much composure here, in order to hold fast to the true thread, and not let her picture become distracted much as the client's own life is being distracted.

Perhaps this sounds very complicated, but it is much helped by a special factor of mediumship. This is the instancy of the medium's insights; to find her client's spiritual whereabouts she does not have to find a way in a kind of emotional Hampton Court maze. (That is more what the client does). The medium's instancy is significant, at times her material comes to her almost of itself, she hardly knows how. The majority of mediums come to know that such a flash arriving without any reference to the words before it, is probably the important thing which will most come home to the client. Much of the task lies in bringing back her recipient more closely towards his own true being.

As F.W.H. Myers has indicated, the time for the old style of evidence largely relating to the former earth personality has been followed for too long, and the main task of mediumship is now to help men and women to recognise more fully the spiritual being they really are. This is obviously an area calling for mediumship of a more refined level than the familiar platform message-giving.

This focus of vision has very far-ranging implications, one of the most important being that a man, whether in the inner world, or on earth, can see only a very little beyond the view afforded by his present spiritual stature. Another is that the over static picture of life in the world after death presented for many years as Spiritualistic dogma is now ripe for enrichment into a more demanding presentation, reaching towards a series of views as perceived from successive steps on the spiritual staircase.

Although each step always brings its own truth and its own limitations individual spiritual work is always involved in reaching towards a deeper vision. The recipient, the listener, the pupil, the struggling pilgrim, is obliged beyond death to find and follow his own path, each by a gradual enlargement of his own consciousness. In the old-fashioned mealy-mouthed phrases a man or woman is 'promoted' on dying and is later 'taken up' to another 'sphere' where he is no longer to be seen by those in the sphere he has recently left behind. If he wishes to show himself to them it is necessary to put on the old 'mask' and 'lower his vibration' to his former companions' levels once more. This over-geographical picture is likely to become superseded in favour of a more inward view. Thus one is not 'promoted' by dying, one arrives with the same familiar imperfect character. The important thing is that the change is less one of place than of consciousness. In early days it is still an earthly time-space concept.

When a philosopher orates, his listeners can usually follow his early distinctions, but then as he embarks on more rarefied ones they can no longer follow these and become lost. He enters upon too deep an area of perception for them. Sometimes, whether on earth or beyond, in an inward way it is possible to receive, from wherever one now stands, just a momentary glimpse of what lies beyond. This is like an act of grace. However brief, it makes a lasting impression. Unlike the philosopher's subtleties the glimpse brings a truth fresh to each recipient, and recognised from within. Some near-death experiences, as reported, partake of this quality.

THE MEDIUM AT WORK: INNER LEVELS

In terms of mediumship, a sensitive is able on a particularly favourable day to raise her own insight to a level above her normal one – usually it reflects the vision of the mentor whose servant she willingly is. This can help to raise the recipient in turn past his present landscape of problems. When Lawrence Temple was given such a spiritual experience, his discarnate teacher told him he had been 'lifted out of the body for a moment, and as a child is lifted, that he may see over a wall that is too high for him'.

When a medium receives such a moment of insight from a higher level, whether derived from depths of her own being or derived from her mentor, she feels very much at one with herself at a deep and largely impersonal level. A considerable degree of compassion is then likely to sharpen her insight. At such times, she may find herself looking deep into the inner aura, regarded here as an aspect of the spiritual self of her client. At such a level, she will not become confused at all with the outer feelings the recipient considers are so important, she is concerned with the area where her client and herself are spiritual beings of equal value, with the full dignity belonging thereby to each. Here the medium finds herself charged with the task of assuming a mantle, which however incompletely she can wear it, belongs at its true depth to that of a priestess. Priest and priestess, like artist, like doctor, like parent and child, are amongst the archetypal roles of human beings. It is sad if basic daily outer selves are allowed to overlay the spiritual values which are required implicitly, if not continuously, in these and other such roles.

How then is the medium to carry out so deep a task? Certainly not to preach nor dogmatise, but to seek the key to the client's situation, perhaps already deposited in the deepest part of the medium's mind by her own mentor. Her task is to focus very clearly upon it, and then find a way to convey it as near to its true level as she senses will be acceptable. Certainly there is no room here for any 'holier than thou' attitude, still less any element of 'allow me to know best'.

If a medium presumes to take on the role of priestess without the qualities it needs, the result will be inflation in the medium and probably in the client also. This is a hazard of the mediumistic profession. Sooner or later all need to find a way to some kind of relationship with the mysterious Universe in which they are contained, and also with their own undisclosed part of the self. That is what a good deal of serious mediumship is really about. Man on earth as a spiritual being is already living in some level of the inner world of spirit, just as surely as he will do so after death. As a teacher once said in speaking of human relationships, 'Always remember the dignity of the spirit'. It is to this spirit in its dignity that mediums can at the right moment address themselves. Too often, unfortunately, they are faced by sitters insistent in attempting to draw them down to a very mundane level at which their gifts cannot work to advantage. The dignity of the spirit which the recipient truly owns is not best reached by flowery phrases; sometimes a piercing realism can dispel illusion much better than easy but cloudy piety. As a medium of high repute has said after her death, a medium's words have to be tailored to the recipient's own present levels of awareness; this is the penalty sometimes patiently paid by the medium for a recipient's non-comprehension. As the recipient moves to deeper levels the tailoring can be more subtle, and the spiritual situation can be discussed more directly.

It is important to realise that the same principle which Maurice Barbanell found and described after his death also belongs just as exactly to life on earth; that each new level of experience requires corresponding enlargement in the vessel which receives it. Else it is not possible fully to participate. The recipient is walking in a world of which the greater part is mentally invisible to him.

THE MEDIUM AT WORK: INNER LEVELS

The advice which a discarnate teacher offers has important similarities to that of transpersonal psychology, aiming to help the student to bring about a degree of personal transformation. If it can be done this way, why then trouble with a discarnate teacher? It depends whether his insight into the pupil's inner nature has a wider background than those of earthly teachers, very valuable and intuitive though these can be. The importance of the discarnate mentor is that he will have larger access to layers of the pupil's past history in earlier lives, his karmic inheritance, in terms of former causes as well as present effects. Because of this he treads where the transpersonal psychologist usually prefers not to enter. The discarnate teacher, if not impeded by the medium, can have a special kindling effect upon the pupil. He sees even more accurately than the medium what words will most wisely guide the pupil towards his next step. He gives hints which at first sometimes seem vague or meaningless until the pupil arouses himself to see beyond the purposely veiled meaning.

Unfortunately the séance room is too often plagued by those who visit a sensitive only for frivolous, ignorant or unworthy reasons. At other times her client is already of some interior substance, one who has both confronted and been confronted by searching problems, and whose feelings of interior loss are at times at a deep level. He is likely in fact to be a senior and worthy recipient, and the sensitive will respond to this. Her task then is to find and draw forth material from spiritual resources already residing in him. She may draw this insight direct from her teacher or from her inner observation of the recipient where as yet unresolved areas of his struggle lie, which he has lost out on or denied, or has not yet fully discovered. Such a recipient probably does not need nor want evidence of survival. The medium is sometimes obliged to find entry in a form not too welcome to the daily outer self of the client. The deep compassion she often feels will overcome any rebuff from her client and she will retain her composure, together with a power of endurance when hurt by her client's occasional insensitive or wilful responses.

She will not find the key by observation or deduction at an intellectual level. This, as she knows, would be insufficient. At times she waits for an inward direction which will urge her insight to a vantage place where the true situation becomes revealed. It does not matter where her spur comes from, what matters is the resonance, the ring of truth it brings to her client. This is one way the sensitive knows when she is on the right track. At her best she finds herself in the telepathic area of wordless and instant communion with her mentor. At other times the meaning can appear in a symbol which instantaneously conveys its own meaning.

It is here no longer a question of being careful not to read the recipient's outer aura. At this level she would have little interest in it because it is an area of agitation, part of the perturbations of the outer personality. At the deeper level, the sensitive can very properly be concerned with the inner aura, which provides as it were a signature tune revealing the individual who lies behind the mask of the enmeshed earthly person. Here lodged within is knowledge of the special tasks which, before returning, he pledged himself to try to carry out during his present life. The sensitive aims to restore to her recipient conscious knowledge of some of this spiritual purpose and so put him further on his right pathway.

This is not to say that the medium will not be called upon at times to wrestle with some of her client's outer disturbances. But all being well, interest in the outer self is gradually left behind by the pupil in order to come to belong more fully to part at least of his total self. Most on earth feel a need to keep hold of the earthly self in an available way. This is healthy enough when not too prolonged, and perhaps forming a respite from effort, a rest from the difficult journey ahead. But of course it will not satisfy for long, nor must it be allowed to mask a truancy. At such times the essence of the medium's insights at their best can remain very pure and undisturbed. If the sensitive constantly moves away from the qualities which belong to this priestess level, then gradually what it is able to tell her will fade away, coming about less and less often, and is likely ultimately to disappear.

CHAPTER EIGHT

SELF-MEDIUMSHIP

MANY HUMANS carry with them a somewhat acute sense of their limitations. In one part of themselves they look towards ways of deepening their outlook and their actions in their desire to become fuller human beings and better in touch with further layers of their private reality. They recognise an ability for this even if it seems faint and distant, but to say 'one day' is not a good excuse. It takes considerable time to come to know that becoming a fuller person often involves discarding as much as acquiring. Myers speaks too of much unlearning to be done after death.

The seer Tudor Pole used to say: 'Every man his own medium'. Such mediumship does not concern itself with mundane affairs. It can be looked upon rather as inwardly bestowed or discovered advice to the spiritual pupil in oneself. It is a field of interior communication. It is least of all concerned with minding other persons' spiritual business. But how, it will be asked, is a recipient to become trained, or train himself, to receive accurately? The first requirement is that he should wish to for its own sake, rather than for his. The second is to accept that it will gradually call for much more spiritual work on himself. This can be at any pace he chooses, but the *effects* are strenuous if he is to come, with its help, to see himself more nearly as he really is, and having seen, to recognise the need for this further work. Whether here or in the post-mortem world, similar tasks confront the pupil, and though they can be postponed, in the end they are unavoidable. At its simplest, self-mediumship represents an ability for occasional telepathy, but at a spiritual level. A spiritual world is touched where men and women, post-mortem or otherwise, are more in tune with all that is around them. This attunement is as sustaining as is the air we breathe whilst on earth.

Self-mediumship, then, performs a different task than that of most professional mediumship. One part of its spiritual background teaches that only a small portion of the whole self comes down into incarnation – the self of everyday is little more than the equivalent of a finger or toe compared with the whole. It is a difficult task gradually to bring into earth consciousness a further fragment of one's true self. If one succeeds, spiritual help is given for the tasks and trials ahead, caused by the incorporation of a further fragment of the whole. Hence in self-mediumship one can encounter parts of one's more valuable being. Former aspects of living, which until now had satisfied one, do so no longer. This will demand a rigorous and alert self-measuring. Here one meets an occult saying: 'No man is your friend, no man is your enemy, each man is your teacher'.

So self-mediumship is basically a form of work upon the self, an exercise in spiritual gardening. It also requires a dedication for service to the world, as does professional mediumship. It is not to be considered as a kind of lesser amateur mediumship, delivering sloppy half-accurate messages of a superficial and imperfectly focussed kind. It is really a process for a different purpose, though it uses a degree of the same inner receptivity and sensitivity as the professional medium. When fully disciplined it is of considerable value.

Self-mediumship in its true form is therefore closely related to communion which the dictionary defines as 'an intimate or sublime exchange of thoughts and feelings'. But with whom, or with what group? One's deep spiritual self does not live as a solitary. Quite certainly the essential intention is to pass beyond the personal boundaries, and to find a path towards the loving and impersonal. If it remains only in the realm of the personal it can often turn out to be no more than attempting to gain a spiritual advantage in an unworthy way.

Self-mediumship does not differ from other ways of mediumship in that it too involves finding a path to an area of stillness, in which the appropriate material gradually finds its own gentle way into the heart. It will be 'heard', but not in the physical ear; it is more like a telepathic rapport in which most or all of the senses are present and play a part though more subtly than when physical. Whilst this is a passive act, how one reacts to the impression will indeed be active though sometimes in an interior way, for what is received has to be put into practice. It is likely to throw light upon a situation or suggest action, not perhaps of a wholly welcome kind. To act with impersonal intent exacts the cost of very pure motives.

Who suggests the thoughts which are received? Other persons, normally but not necessarily discarnate, or it can come from a pool of thought, or simply (and often unwelcome) from oneself. The fact that a thought is identified as coming from an inward part of oneself does not at all exclude the equally important fact that it can have been put there earlier by a mentor for gestation, or received during sleep, emerging later into the conscious self.

In fact to assume that one acts largely as an isolated being and can take credit for having created the entire contents of one's own mind is an illusion not countenanced at all in the inner world. Man certainly does not live for himself alone. All serious connection with the inner world involves an area of coming together with others, even when not fully recognised.

A certain paradox arises here. As most sensitives recognise, and most creative artists as well, an area of silence is the productive place for the entry of new thoughts, feelings and perceptions. By silence is meant conscious entry into an area in which all one's local interest and perturbances sink into irrelevance and disappear, bringing one into a unity never known before, a deep seriousness which gives birth also to a joy in the existence of others.

Within the silence many levels reside, from a stillness where creative perceptions find a way into the daily world, to a much more shallow and precarious listening only a shade below the normal noisy surface, and inevitably tainted by one's near presence, or by imperfect motives. Self-mediumship, when at its best, can be accurate, useful and pertinent; it is rather like the working insight of a friend. If it becomes over-confident it will probably come only from oneself and be entirely wrong. At its best self-mediumship can gradually pass into a spiritual communion, or a contemplative area of spiritual values. Impersonal integrity of judgment is an essential tool.

The professional medium can sometimes touch closely these areas on behalf of her client. It then remains his duty to obey the disciplines needed to lay firm hold of the medium's offered insights and set to work to deepen his own path. Humility is required to recognise where lies the present right truth for him and to recognise that merely personal preferences of taste and opinion no longer matter.

The path of self-mediumship can be a positive and healthy one. It is not to be regarded as the lot of a medium *manquée*, although some of its aspects can be such. As with full mediumship, success is very much in scale with the personal disciplines achieved.

The practice of self-mediumship sometimes proves to be a degree of apprenticeship before full mediumship is reached, in that the type of discipline is to some degree the same for each. The problem is for the self-medium to recognise where the nub of the self-discipline really lies at each stage. It includes becoming aware of and acknowledging when the source lies only in the medium's conscious self. It is easy to prefer to tell oneself the source is discarnate. This is the self-medium's characteristic trap, that of self-delusion.

In most ways, the self-medium has the easier lot. She will less often have to face the failures and weaknesses of character which a full medium perceives in her clients, and which too often the client fails to have the wish to check. This brings with it much pain to the serious medium.

Where the self-medium falls short of the full medium in technique is in some way or another a lack of ability to allow her communicator an unimpeded message. Constantly her own values and concepts, her own life-style, intrude because she lacks the volatility to let go; they remain the clumsy heavy luggage which has for too long impeded her journey. By letting go, the full medium is enabled to grow in her work, allowing the communicator's deeper voice to be heard by her. Her temperament too allows her a natural power of dissociation, her auric antennae are less tightly contained, and this is why her task is both easier and more difficult than that of the self-medium who has less natural ability to start with.

Therefore it is usually wise for the self-medium to limit herself to tasks which lie within her natural range. She will then find herself led towards spiritually disciplined perceptions which will steadily deepen her being. She will indeed find she has plenty to do in work upon herself before she dies!

Self-mediumship can readily be seen to be something of a hybrid discipline. It is overlapped by full mediumship on one side, and often by religious dogmas on the other. The common temptation for the self-medium is to spread her wares too widely, gradually developing her gift in order to provide advice to one or two friends, and then a few others until a small group gradually forms itself around her. This inevitably becomes a coterie group, and the leader finds herself called upon to answer questions on very varied subjects. Since many of these will lie outside the area of her true

SELF-MEDIUMSHIP

sensitivity the answers begin to flow simply from knowledge and opinions she has, or has read from other teachers, about which she certainly has no qualifications to teach. A coterie usually turns into a dangerous encumbrance; it is also an area into which communicators of ill-will all too often seek to enter, elevating the original humble servant of truth into a victim of personal inflation.

The opposite danger is of course if she selfishly decides to use the fruits of her meditation only for herself and deny them to others. There can be misers beside those with material riches they will never spend; the coin can be in spiritual terms, sometimes denying any value to others' spiritual earnings, and craving for themselves realms likely to lead them into megalomania. Both these pitfalls are obviously not often so extreme, but to gradually come to stand on such ground is very unsound.

These dangers are avoided when it is always borne in mind that self-mediumship combines the role of sensitive and recipient, and the double discipline can prove a good safeguard. If conveying to another what is taken to be the voice of one's own mentor, to speak in terms of over-certainty or of pressurising provide sure danger-signals.

If one is mainly reflecting one's own higher or inner self, this will be impersonal and not self-interested, and will speak at deeper than personality level. It is not difficult to know when the inner self is truly speaking, which will be in terms of friendly insight, and will probably point out any needed areas of discipline in one's own being. Else self-importance and vanity are likely to creep in. It is a good question to ask whether one is keeping one's own council to good advantage. Just as spiritual knowledge resides in the silence, so the recipient will often do well to observe it in turn. It is not difficult to become aware if one is proving a lazy or disobedient servant to one's inner voice, but of considerable difficulty to overcome the fault.

There are times when one's mentor needs to be given the opportunity of speaking from a perhaps different angle through an independent spiritual medium. The message then will often be found to be deeper and much better focussed than the one formerly imbibed from within oneself.

What is required, and required to be recognised, is the need for constant obedience, but of course it has to be to the right voice. To find that advice is steadily isolating one from other views, including commonsense ones, is another very clear danger signal.

Self-mediumship must never compete with the larger function of mentor-produced teaching. A better word for self-mediumship would be inner awareness, which more correctly defines its function and setting. It needs and is a quest for a positive and supportive spiritual philosophy, for oneself and occasionally to support others too. Above all self-mediumship must never claim proprietary rights for what it imparts; such insights as it touches on, just because they are insights, will also be observed by others on similar wavelengths, though sometimes expressed in different terms.

The one who practises self-mediumship successfully will be a member of a team in the inner world all of whom she does not yet know, and which is working at deeper levels than her own; she will be a junior member.

Trust is a necessity. A mentor is likely to say: trust us, trust yourself. The need is to find where and what one needs to trust – the right part of it, at the right time, towards the right teacher and at all times trust in the spiritual law. Evil communicators also demand trust but only in order to mislead.

Like some other true disciplines, that of self-mediumship does not consist of a set of rules, it relates to all within the inner life of the pupil, and is to be learned slowly through the effects of the discipline itself. It relates to many parts of living. It is in fact a simple form of the classical religious discipline to lose oneself, but gentler in underlying severity. It does not command a vow, and much will be taught to the pupil by himself, for he learns what intensifies and gives precision to his insights, and what only leads to some form of indulgence.

A true mentor though always kind, is also rigorous and exact. A false mentor, that is to say a deceiver, throws dust in a listener's eyes by assuring him of having already achieved many virtues he has never, or insufficiently, worked for, and by putting a world of glamour into his hands.

Such illusion can be readily present in some too easily acquired 'channelling' today. Each listener needs to ask himself seriously where the words are really pointing; are they drawn from piercing insight, or do they glitter but point nowhere? The loftier they seem, the more opportunity for glitter without substance.

In England counselling is an activity requiring a long training and a subsequent role of professional status and discipline. Its title should not be used by others, least of all those working as mediums. Some of these describe their work loosely as counselling when it includes the mere giving forth of their own uninstructed personal opinion, in short practising as a medium when they are often not functioning as one.

The most extensive counselling is carried out in America, claiming to represent the view of exalted discarnate teachers, of whom counsellor and client get to know very little. The name he gives is taken as authority, rather than the contents of his words. In England a distance is always present between medium and mentor. The medium does not work alongside her teacher but very much as one under his direction.

American counselling, or channelling as it is now usually called, lies outside the range of this book. It is impossible not to observe however its assured tone, and without it perhaps counsellors would find it hard to make a way as an acknowledged teacher. There is however no gainsaying that many counsellors are certainly without the many years of disciplined work which English mediums feel it necessary to observe before their work reaches its full maturity, and which require a considerable discipline in the medium's own character.

True self-mediumship too certainly needs more exacting work than non-professional channelling, into which too much of the operating personality enters; it is basically part of the same discipline which the full medium is called upon to observe if she wishes to give herself completely to working with and for a mentor.

It cannot be overlooked that counsellors need to remember that ease of acquiring is also often a guide to its value. A considerable amount of easily acquired channelling readily on offer is miles apart from what long years of disciplined mediumship is able to produce. Mediumship is certainly in course of changing and so may its disciplines: these disciplines, in new or old form, will always be its hallmark. The laws of karma are not to be overturned.

What if a teacher is false? The contents, just because they are new will be hard to judge; the words spoken in what is claimed to be new, tend to be glamorous, and it is wise to regard them with suspicion. However it would be churlish to deny the possibility of a new exhilaration which can draw us forward in a right way calling for a joyous trust which will then find itself in harmony with the arrival of a new outpouring of spirit. Trouble comes if we greet it with the wrong qualities in ourselves.

At times the impulse appears to take away as much as it gives. The classical disciplines cannot be dismissed or ignored. Whatever their change their essence will remain. What appears out of date or even wrong and chaining lies in the dogma and behaviour which in all religions have gradually been introduced and allowed to ossify the original impulse. It is certainly a feature of the new impulses that the corners of one's mouth should not be allowed to turn down so continually at what one sees in others and which is different from one's self.

SELF-MEDIUMSHIP

One teacher declares that man's outer personality is nothing more than a picture made by his own observation, as is similarly everything else he sees around him. This somewhat extreme view can help towards some useful reorientation but would seem, by implication, to limit the teacher himself similarly. It produces two very considerable difficulties. The first is that in this view the value of love as the most creative of all expressions largely disappears. The second difficulty is that it gives little value to earth as a divine creation, or to the force which has created and sustains it.

It is surely not in the very least likely that basics, like the gifts of love and the role of teachers, will disappear or assume little value. Though their mode may change, their fundamental purpose surely will not. To call for the throwing away of familiar concepts requires something better with which to replace them. If no love appears in the picture it must be wrong somewhere. If the words seem fair the substance behind them can be very different. Unless what the teacher brings resonates in a sure way to the inner in ourselves, his real purpose must remain suspect. If attempting to destroy a familiar pathway is he replacing it with one which leads nowhere? The listener's own integrity as always must be the judge. To take steps into the unknown is a serious matter.

The Kingdom of Heaven is within. Of course it is not the glamorous thing it may sound. If one comes to claim that one's limitations have been cast off, it can be no more than that one has ceased to observe them at work. It is quite certain that whatever qualities one ascribes to the within, the pupil cannot be a mere poacher of others' spoken words. It is one's actions afterwards which really count. When found the new has then to be grown further.

The whole complex of new teaching in future mediumship will at first fall most on the young and mid-generations. It is impossible to know on which step of the Jacob's Ladder one is at present standing, and hence how wide a consciousness one can reach. It is an act of egotism to ask and to want to know. Does one dare to begin to teach all who care to come along? This needs first a long and exacting look at oneself.

If the pupil thinks the discipline is to be swiftly gained the usual end is self-glorification. The results of self-mediumship are bound up with the discipline or non discipline practised, and are therefore bound to reflect it. A serious attitude, but with some humour, is a good discipline in itself. If one really wants self-mediumship in order to display it to others, then clearly there is insufficient discipline. The channel needs to be cleared constantly and steadily.

CHAPTER NINE

THE MENTOR

1

TO SUMMARISE, it is necessary to recognise that most external factual tests designed to evaluate on the one side mediumistic performance, or on the other to show up mediumship as a delusion, are largely irrelevant at deeper levels of communication. Fact checking has little or nothing to do with any spiritual realisation, and needs to be confined to its proper role. The best way to discover whether value exists in apparent spiritual communication is to see if it works on earth. As we have seen there is no need to be dependent only on a medium. Communion continues to be available to the sensitive listener outside the mediumistic interview, in a controlled and growing way, quite unrelated to spontaneous evidence of the crisis type. Fundamentally it is a growing recognition of what one's own nature is waiting to tell of itself and of inner and outer worlds.

Obviously there is a difference between the early contacts made with the help of a sensitive, and later ones in an altogether deeper field. Early communications, because of unfamiliarity with the difficult communications process at both ends of the line, sometimes end in disappointment. Like other things communication needs practice and familiarity. Later more significant contacts convey a strong sense of beings who are present, who whilst giving little information concerning themselves, are able to talk with evident familiarity and affection about the most private areas in their listener. Such marks the arrival of a mentor, one who gradually becomes recognised as an experienced and trusted friend and adviser. The task of mentors is not to issue homilies, but to bring a deeper awakening. They show they already know of the issues of present concern to their listener. They are sharing and caring, communicating warmth and encouragement. They may suggest a course to take but never impose it. More often they discuss a change in feeling-tones within the situation which then throws quite a different light on it to their pupil. A sense of a wider vision than one's own conveys itself. Their evident concern imparts with it a sense both of their reality and their independence from both sensitive and listener.

Why should they take an interest? They establish to us that we exist in a life of wider scale and longer time-span than only on earth. They are seen as companions in this deeper existence to which each gradually begins to find he or she already belongs. It can be a very long and heartening encounter.

The mentor, like man himself, has a double task, in facing this two-fold nature; the so-called natural man in close mesh with this earth, and the spiritual man whose task it is to create both himself and his own fragment of earth life in its true and intended shape.

Dante, in a famous passage of the *Divine Comedy*, pictured himself in his mid-years making his way through a dark wood. The symbol holds an extended meaning for modern life.

First of course it represents the Jungian mid-life situation but also a hidden picture of a man's own past lives, the effects of which continue to lie heavy upon and within him. Mentors teach reincarnation as a fact; it is an essential tool. The natural and so obstinate person we have made of ourselves during our earth life to date is related to experiences in former lives. Now we have been returned to life and given opportunities to overcome our own past creations, which present themselves again because so far unregenerated. The mentor has attached his pupils to himself because of his deep and long knowledge of their past. He comes to share in order to lend a helping hand in the long task still remaining. Without help, old passions, still alive and the results of former choices, would be likely to cause the pupil to dig himself more deeply into the mire. The mentor in a very real sense bears our lot, in order that we can succeed in bearing it better ourselves. This is why the quality they most often enjoin is patience. With patience it becomes better seen what is so necessary to eradicate. It takes time to understand what old deeds represent. They can be very tenacious and it can require more time still to recognise the deep tangle brought about in the character. If each asks himself what is his real quality of character and then looks deeply and honestly within, he is likely to find its own opposite also lies there almost as fully but behind the surface. The mentor helps the pupil to penetrate this façade. Suppose for instance that one is confident of being an extremely fair-minded person. But have we looked at both best and worst? Actions deplored in others quite likely conceal excellent qualities. If confident we ourselves are generous souls, where does our well-lit generosity end, and give way to ill-lit meanness? Generosity in one set of terms can march along with meanness in another. What of the head of the family, so generous to all he meets, so caring for those in poverty yet who keeps his own family somewhat short so as to stand well in his neighbours' eyes and in his own? Where does a loyalty, well advertised to oneself, suddenly come to an end, forsaking another's need by making judgment just when the loyalty is most tested and needed?

Relics of past character can thus germinate afresh in present life; they can also relate to other quarters of the character, in terms not as yet recognised. A man leaves off drunkenness perhaps and his struggle is hard and genuine. But what of the recklessness and heedlessness which induced it in the first place, and could well remain and replace the drunkenness by some equally undesirable activity?

Known or unknown, within the character or the circumstances, there will be found limned this continuation of faults from other lives, having fruits now still present precisely because we have formerly failed to deal with them and now find them grown beyond their former size, for nothing stands still. If it does not decline then it grows.

To quote one mentor:

> You find it difficult to believe that the sickness, loneliness or tribulation you suffer is the result of your own soul's wish, But it is so. Never blame other people for your troubles. Always look within ... then the reason for the condition which limits you will become clear, and you will see the work you have to do within yourself.

Thus outer troubles, seemingly so unfair, very frequently relate, in one way or another, to a source within oneself. That is why they make so strong a reverberation, so unrelenting an impact. Other events seeming to others to be much worse, can be easily sustained because that is not where one's particular debt to life arises. Individual circumstances are usually painting a picture of part of past and present selves, so that we can see better. Of course it is not always easy to see the meaning of the picture. That is where individual effort comes in. The qualities found so trying in others, even those whom we deeply love bear a relation somewhere to us also. For its possessor the significance will probably be of a different kind. In the telling phrase, he *suffers* that quality. Suffering is a product of the faults of ourselves and others, writ perhaps in

THE MENTOR

larger letters than before so as to enable it to show itself so clearly now as to affirm without doubt that *something must be done*. Misfortune and failure create opportunity. Suffering is not to be blamed on others because behind it is justice bringing about its own.

It cannot be said too often that reincarnation is not punitive in intention. Here is where we spiritually stand, until we recreate our bruised and fractured characters. Reincarnation offers the opportunity to become otherwise. This is justice through and through: it is also love. The mentor stands by to point the way to the action which will release us. It is we who lose patience, the mentor does not. The mentor then comes to us because we are deep in the dark wood of ourself. His purpose is to help and it is not at all to please us with evidence about himself. Evidence belongs to the outer personality. The mentor also does not offer it since his life no longer lies within an outer personality. It is true that since it is necessary to show himself to us in an outer form, he assumes a character of some kind, probably from his own past, likely to be one strongly exhibiting some characteristic of special value to us at present. He selects it for the task in hand. He does not primarily encourage in us a personal relationship with his assumed self. He is content to say: 'Remember I am only a thought away from you'.

Similarly his task is to help us overcome things in us of which we have no further need. Not too interested in the pupil's personal self, he talks largely instead to the inner self about its present problems. The pupil, of course, also bears within him qualities he has already grown which lead him nearer to his own true being. These are his main working tools to help weed out his imprisoning qualities. Some of his true attributes he only possesses potentially as yet. They are infant qualities. He possibly thinks he has them in full strength. The mentor, surveying the length and depth of his knowledge of all the qualities the pupil has allowed to grow in his former lives, and of his struggles in the inner worlds between, can see precisely where lies the true point of growth. It would go quite against the facts to assume the mentor only sees and knows the present guise of his pupil, which is only a small part of his full self. Today's selection, as it were. The mentor is well aware of deeper qualities at present playing only a preliminary role in his pupil. The view of the mentor is long term.

2

Clearly this relationship of mentor and pupil is a very special one. It differs somewhat from the traditional stern guru-chela disciplines of the East. It is based on love and insight. Long before the present life span, the mentor will already have taken the pupil to his heart. The love, though positive, is never indulgent. Here it differs from much human love. If it is said that he is always on our side, it does not in the least mean that he deceives himself about us. It is that in a remarkable way he sees at the same moment our problems both as we see them and as he sees them. His true concern lies in what is important for our future. This can be very different from what our present limitations cause us to wish for.

The mentor is often content, out of his love, to speak in a personal way, for he knows that this reassures us. One task the pupil needs to learn is to distinguish this tone from the different tone when he is speaking at a level of more impersonal spiritual recognition. The guide's warmth plays creatively on both levels. A worthy pupil always listens, though he may not yet fully understand. At times, by a kind of sleight of hand, the mentor slips in a comment or piece of advice which the outer self of the pupil would be likely to resist, much as the language of dreams bypasses the resistant censor in the waking self. The guide has a rather similar intention. He is content to wait for the seed to germinate. Gradually and in various ways he tries to encourage the pupil to think and to live in more lasting terms, so that he becomes less his own slave.

On a broader canvas, the encouragement to the pupil is to create or reveal true qualities of character not by introspective fuss or over-scrupulosity, but simply by going out and *being* them, and going on being them.

As the pupil becomes aware of how very far he still has to go before becoming his full spiritual self, he gradually gains the detachment to recognise that the now familiar image of his mentor is a scaled-down version geared to the pupil's own limitations. The mentor he knows is easier for him to listen to; were he to function in his full being, much would lie outside the reach of the pupil's perception. Probably he would then not even be aware of the presence of the mentor who needs to assume a persona as part of what the discarnate world calls 'the blessed limitation' of earth life. To the mentor, earth life takes place in perpetual slow motion. As one said: 'Imagine a bulb in a pot, watch the slow rise of the shoots and the gradual forming and emergence of its flower. That is how one of your earth questions appears to us, between thought and speech.'

3

Many recipients, especially intellectuals, allow themselves to fall deeply into Blake's 'cloudy doubts and reasoning cares', where objective proof is sought as being of more value than personal experience or than any different category of values arising from interior sources. The mentor makes it possible to begin afresh to trust experience more despite appearances seemingly to the contrary, and to begin to find life worthy of an essential optimism.

INNER EYE, LISTENING EAR

Men think of the inner life beyond death in too linear a way; earth conditions them to this. The more we study, we realise how little we know of how things come about in the inner world. An important new factor comes into view, that our inner self is already a greater and more important part of us, whether recognised or not. We know little of how it influences us. We can however come to see there is a link between the two modes of living. The mentor is part of the link. During the hours of sleep too, we are told, opportunities exist to learn, or to re-learn, or simply to recognise. Occasionally we succeed in translating some of these intimations into our waking life. However vague and slender our grasp on them we begin gradually to enrich the quality of our living. One teacher refers to this inner self as the captain of the ship, sending down orders. Nothing effective is achieved only by talking or listening, only by doing and being.

The mentor imparts to us directly through a medium and indirectly by intuition and other subtle impulses which we can lay hold of during our waking life. The true links lie on the inner side of life. By making too many demands upon the mentor concerning worldly matters, it makes his proper work more difficult, and can result in paying too much attention to the animal in man who then sometimes rides his owner rather than vice-versa.

The world is against us, in that we cannot wholly go against its pace. The inner world on the contrary is in our favour. It is our home, even now on earth. Mentor and medium and pupil alike are obliged to work in the hurly-burly of crude mass emotions which have invaded areas properly belonging to the inner world, bringing into it conflicts and confusions.

The Ancient Egypt temple life was a place in which the neophyte could learn to use body and mind, heart and spirit in tune with the inner world, and it guarded its pupils from the turbulences of the outer world. At present the pupil has to create and enter his private inner temple. In Ancient

Egypt, before men and women in the outer world came to the Temple for help, a dedicated priestess would already have studied their soul in the inner world and would know just what spiritual advice was now needed. Some of this help may indeed have already been given in converse between them during sleep and would then be repeated in earth terms. The task of the priestess or medium would have been easier then than now, where information carried in the peaceful world has to emerge into and penetrate earth confusion here. The medium can be much helped by a pupil bringing what he possesses of achieved silence to help harmony and peace to come together more fully into the areas hopefully to be shared in their sessions.

4

Authority is a dangerous master. The essence of true discarnate communication lies in its openness. Because it is free it can be offered at many levels. Not all is sweetness and light. Dark beings of evil intent, and trivial-minded mischief-makers can appear and need to be assessed as their true purpose discloses itself. Such communicators are not in the mainstream; these criminals and strayed folk must be ignored, and not listened to. The first attempts to free oneself from such attacks lie in remembering that the assaults are invariably made upon weaknesses they perceive in one's own character. As for the majority of communicators, on the contrary, a transparent sense of good will is a marked characteristic; it is part of their inner well-being which transmits itself so unmistakably, whether they are normal men and women who tried to do the best they could on earth, or someone of deeper achievement. What has become different is their expanded horizon behind this unflagging energy of good will. Life after death sustains them in a deep way. How can this be known? By the vitality and light which comes so often with their words, or impinges directly upon the recipient's own inner senses.

As one becomes more accustomed to communication it will be observed, as indeed would be expected, that there are different grades and calibres in those who truly come to help. The listener gravitates more to certain of them. It begins to be felt that one's peers and companions offer general good companionship. Then there are what might be called intermediary figures, obedient to their own seniors and who play a very useful role in sowing the seed. True mentors establish a deeper more intimate note. The recipient feels in time that he belongs to a spiritual group. Something of a common language of spiritual values establishes itself. Behind such a group there can be expected one who is teacher to the whole group, to whom all in the group look up. He may indeed, though seldom, make a direct appearance, as it were on a special feast day.

At an ordinary level those with a slight degree of telepathic sensitivity are likely to have an occasional experience, probably lasting only a few moments, of being under spiritual scrutiny. One feels the presence of a keenly insightful and deeply kind being. This is probably one's own mentor. One is less likely to sense what the being looks like. If there is no sequel, one is probably regarded as in need of further deepening experience in the next few earth years ahead. No sense of failure is felt; simply that spurs are not yet won.

Whatever the grade of communication, a common factor will be seen: the communicator assesses our readiness for response. It is also as if we begin to sense somewhere within us a locked-up store of knowledge of our own; tools of which we have somehow lost the use. The mentors are attempting to re-awaken these. Their companionship is therefore of serious import, and if we respond, then gradually we are drawn into whatever pattern best serves. It is possible of course to turn one's back on the invitation. Many do, either deliberately, or because more and more engulfed by everyday necessities or pleasures. It requires some faith to accept a new pattern.

What then makes this material worthy of a deep response? The pupil comes to feel in an unmistakable way a private insight into his being both deeper and more sure than his own. This presents itself to him for scrutiny by his present insights. It offers an awakening. This has important implications. It is more spiritually costly to live by a larger layer of being, than in the familiar limited everyday world. It forms a challenge, needing to be constantly repeated until listened to. To make a new set of values one's own requires a remoulding of attitude to many familiar situations, and often a gradual moving away from some of them. Once a serious attempt is being made, communicators introduce a very positive view of man on earth, as a being upon whom the spirit world is ever showering its own virtues. His horizons are thus enlarged. A familiarity with his larger inner self is being steadily brought about; he is gradually becoming a different being. A warning note needs to be uttered here; his possession of this new being will still be incomplete. There will remain shallows where he is only able to see with his former eyes. There will also be indefinite areas in his levels of perception; he will still be far from living fully within the new man awaiting him.

The worst danger, however, is that he will begin to assume a superiority he is very far from possessing. If he did possess it he would not speak of it. In short, in presenting himself to others he can lead himself into becoming inflated, lowering his stature in doing so.

5

A struggle still continues between his inner self and the familiar natural man enjoying his old environment; he occasionally reaches out in search of his spiritual self, but like a dog at the end of a chain he all too frequently returns to old concerns. In time one will come to sit much more loosely towards former needs. There will come about a growing detachment towards old values. It becomes recognised that the body is also the temple of the spirit, and that whilst the physical body is made of earth and belongs to it and will be cast off with relief, yet it is also a creation of the God force, a ground for serious spiritual work.

The natural values in the traditional life patterns are for enjoyment as well as for lessons, they are not to be regarded as villains on the scene. The natural and the spiritual worlds after all are both part of the same creation. The disciplines of earth certainly offer avenues of enrichment to the spiritual self, can indeed contribute much to it. It is a poor compliment to its Creator to dismiss earth as of little value.

The spiritual self is hard to speak of, both because it is often obscured by the demands of the natural man and because the perceptions needed to know of it are only slowly learned. It is best kept as a large and loosely defined area. When cast into tight intellectual concepts, these can easily cause experience to shrivel. The spiritual needs to be reached on its own terms. Man has to perform a weaning task upon himself.

6

There appears to be a mysterious process in the inner world where some of the events of preceding lives on earth are absorbed into the spiritual self. The essence of these life lessons, their spiritual fruitage and their losses become stored up in one's innermost, to be available for later encounter in fresh earthly endeavours. This innermost temple of the self is sometimes named the seed atom or the causal self. Within it the results of many earth innings are shown upon one's score sheet. These innings have ended and in one sense exist no more. In another sense the score sheet within the spiritual self tells what needs to be produced or continued in future earth innings. Would not all really wish to learn the real meanings of the stories we have lived out, and seek to follow the purposeful threads of continuity therein? The causal self is no dead record, no mere thumbed pages of memories. These lives will be causally related to one another, offering opportunity to fill gaps, and to re-shape characteristics hitherto misused. They point towards the tree of the future growing out of the seed of the past. It is part of the mentor's task to reflect these to his reincarnated pupils.

What then lies at the very centre of the spiritual self and forms its essence? Spiritual teachers, looking far back into the beginning of creation, speak of a spark sent forth from the God force into matter, there to bring about through labour and experience over many thousands of years the individual perfection embedded into it from the God force at its very moment of creation. It is a prospect both frightening and glorious. It is also a picture given to our present as yet miniscule consciousness upon which to build. Such a picture given to us is of course graded to each man's present self.

7

It has been suggested that a good way in which to handle information concerning occult things is not to try and make them too cut and dried, but to regard any advances in truth as no more than approximate, part of a picture which has to remain incomplete. Keats in a famous letter speaking of his own groping from one dark chamber of the soul to a further one, was pointing to a true mode of learning, that one can only learn what one is as yet equipped to learn, but which by learning will then increase the capacity to learn more.

INNER EYE, LISTENING EAR

Mentors often make statements of a kind which put into our hands one end of a thread. If we pull the thread sharply towards us, because we want to possess it whole, it will break off. The better course is to feel one's way gradually along the thread; we then find ourselves able in time to follow it into hitherto hidden chambers.

Mentors thus speak, when it is the right time, of material long locked up in the pupil's store of ancient memories. This is less likely to be in terms of outer facts than an essence which stirs up his conscience. He responds by recognising that he has to find where some now needed action is awaiting him, or to acquire something new, or to put something right. He cannot yet be master in his own house as long as many of its rooms remain locked up. The mentor holds the keys and hands each one over when the pupil is ready. He lights up the pupil's house room by room and only very gradually, for at every turn the pupil is tested for how he deals with the contents he finds.

The occult, however seemingly simple in its form, is not for those who like to rush their fences. That is one reason why it is occult. Different temperaments are suited to different methods of learning. It must not be thought that all mentors work exclusively in occult terms. Some seem to find it best to feed the pupil with very simple ethical suggestions, all of which can be carried out in the everyday world. However simple, they certainly test in many ways the pupil's perseverance and his honesty towards himself. Other temperaments resent the existence of a mentor; each wanting to be his own man. Indeed it is necessary to make his own decisions, but it is not necessary to refuse all help. Experience through the ages repeats the individual or group teacher-pupil relationship in one form or the other. Why be ashamed of still needing a teacher? Education at whatever level is after all one of the noble professions. In spiritual areas, a great deal is given in hints or instructions of which the pupil has to find out the true meaning, as distinct from the obvious one. Pythagorean maxims are an example. 'Do not step over the beam of a balance' and 'do not turn round at the border when you travel abroad'.

In the simple occult forms discussed here the mentor is willing to teach the pupil at a very early stage, sometimes when still fairly fully enmeshed in the outer world, but with a spiritual restlessness as yet hardly understood. Part of the mentor's own sacrifice is to be misunderstood and misrepresented in the need to talk of the pupil's spirituality in everyday terms the pupil can understand.

The requirements of the intellectual temperament are somewhat in conflict with how the mentor most often operates. An occult picture is built up gradually, rather than in one complete view. The intellectual says, why use blunt tools when one has precision tools to hand? He likes to say: either it is thus, or it is not thus. But it is very much an occult maxim that what is true at one level of consciousness is seen to have a different meaning at another level; then the earlier level fades from view since it is no longer required. In obedience to this process a mentor will be found to go on speaking at an acceptable level whether outer or inner, in accordance with his pupil's needs.

8

Why has the theme of reincarnation been steadily introduced by most discarnate mentors with its complex implications, including the highly important one that we are engaged in untying knots with others, as well as knots within oneself? We bear the deposit of many lives within us, lived at different levels and awaiting our resolving of them. In one earth life we bring only a section for immediate attention. More, we are told, would make the burden too great. This is a further reason why man on earth cannot know his whole self. He has quite enough of a problem in dealing with the small section here. Frances Banks, a nun and a deeply spiritual communicator, tells of how she gradually rejoins more of her total self, and with it regains knowledge of many humiliating failures in her former lives.

In the texture of the spiritual teaching of mentors many deep issues arise. Different strands sometimes seem contradictory. Some of these contradictions lessen once they are seen as differing views from separate steps on the spiritual staircase. Others can take us into mystical areas. The deeper we delve, the more complex the nature of the self, yet as mentors tell us also it is the quest for utmost simplicity of being and purpose which in the end makes us most truly ourselves.

One deep question which appears is whether the true human unit is made up of a single being. Is it, so to say, no more than an idealised and complete version of the imperfect person we know, or partly know, here? Mentors are introducing the idea of the group soul. This presentation brings about a cluster of questions. We hear about joining our spiritual group. Are our own past selves still present within the group, to some degree independent of our present self? Some mediums prefer to consider that these past lives are really those of independent beings, who hand on to us the next part of a common task on which they worked, and which we now have to take forward, and so what we regard as our own earlier incarnations were really the lives of these predecessors. This theory of serial lives is one not to be lightly dismissed: it can well be a facet of a deeper truth than can wholly be satisfactorily understood from present levels.

However this may be, others prefer to focus on being part of a spiritual group with a common spiritual aim, held together by a leader of elevated status, a kind of spiritual father. Taking a name at random, how would you, for instance, value finding St Francis is the spiritual father of your group, and probably of many other groups? Wherever one looks, eventually one finds oneself in difficulties with concepts we are barely able to glimpse, and more and more find them to be only a scaled down approximation. Certainly there are always problems awaiting us. For instance husband and wife are maybe told they are part of the same soul. How many others are part of it? Does 'soul' mean 'group', or something closer still? The idea of a twin soul is dear to the human heart. One strong level of teaching implies the final unit is the androgyne, with male and female aspects at last fused into one after many experiences, some still far ahead. One or two communicators, shortly after death, speak of now finding it sometimes difficult to distinguish the sex of those they meet. Elizabeth Haich, on the other hand, speaks of the twin as that part of us which is not at present incarnated. Then again, some mentors speak of another soul as one's affinity, as distinct from twinship. Perhaps affinity is best regarded as a *simplifying* word, one which covers many degrees and depths of spiritual closeness. Should mentors then be written off as untrustworthy if they seem to contradict one another? All the world religions both agree with and also contradict one another, and each has substantial validity of its own. So with mentors, who speak to the condition and level of the pupil. It is possible to write off one ideal as more shallow and incomplete than another, but no mentor would ever condemn an idea for being incomplete. Incomplete it may be, but then who judges? It is very essential that the deeper the teaching appears and the more we are drawn towards it, the more it is also very necessary to keep a respectful distance, to recognise we are simply not yet equipped to understand; that often we cannot as yet reach closer, that the deeper aspects in all their fullness are at present far beyond us. Conceptualising too soon results in a hardening and crystallising process which imprisons us, instead of releasing us to a still wider landscape of knowledge. It is wiser to learn to live in the best harmony we can with apparent irreconcilables, perhaps for a long time. So in this book, firm answers are sometimes lacking, just perhaps where some readers will most hope for them.

In the deeper part of the field, it is irrelevant whether teaching comes from one's own inner self, or from one's mentor, from experience in former lives or from former earth companions, so long as it is true for us to use at the present moment. Teachers are undoubtedly engaged in gradually presenting a wider picture of life and of human selfhood. It is a process of clearing the decks, of unloosening ropes which, more than we are aware, still bind us fast.

How far is the extended perception of mediums able to speak to her client's inner self, which by most definitions already possesses some of the insight needed for fruitful help with the particular problems facing the small part of itself on earth? If a client is able to reach regularly through meditation a degree of access to the deeper inner self, then it becomes easier also for a priestess type of medium to speak the right words. Unlike most professional counsellors, she can sometimes see where causes of some of her client's predicaments lie in karmic inheritance from former lives. But this is nothing to do with glib assumptions from the medium's working stock of familiar ideas.

A priestess medium has to lay aside much of her self to be in tune, and by no means only when she is working. She needs a strict and continuing discipline in living her daily life. Here is her difference from the ordinary platform medium, whose material is largely relayed at the astral level in which most live for a while soon after death, and can be expressed at everyday levels. For some recipients, of course, the soul levels already operate in deep ways, in areas of dedication, of deep love, of selflessness. The astral-based medium will not be able to help these.

THE MENTOR

Lofty-sounding general spiritual pronouncements, fashionable today, and pleasurable to the ego, are no substitute for insight brought to the individual sitter. Those mediums who value their pronouncements as high spirituality really may simply have their feet off the ground. The mystic's cloud of unknowing is much to be preferred to these mediums' cloud of knowing. Communication as time goes on – though everyday evidence will continue – will be looking beyond this for spiritual teaching and for encouraging the client to reach direct intuitive perception of his own. It is certainly possible to hope for greater and more frequent depth in discarnate teachers and also for some growth in direct telepathic communion with one's mentor. Regarding peers, insights may arise, or be given, into past lives in which we and they have been involved together. Here some mediumistic reticence and discretion is necessary. Mentors are beginning to talk a bit more about our past relationships in earlier lives, some with souls with whom there is a permanent though changing and deepening relationship. Thus the son in one life may be the lover in another, and then a brother or sister. It is wise to be especially cautious in talk of exclusive man-woman love relationships over many lives. This can obviously all too easily be a field for glamour.

Mentors can often see fresh problems ahead for pupils seeking greater fullness of being, and the beginnings on earth of living more fully in spiritual dimensions of relationships. In the future, the *balance of emphasis* is likely to become different as we are gradually able to incorporate more of our whole being into the everyday earthly self, and recognise the same process in others. Here one must say realism is essential in order to kick easy uplift downstairs, and fully to accept that deep communication is not only with others, it is also with ourselves.

This calls for recognition of how important and searching long-term relationships can be. They are complex because of

INNER EYE, LISTENING EAR

the intricate karmic patterns involved. To get to the bottom of these includes the facing of compulsive entanglements still tying us to other people, which we ourselves helped to bring about a very long time ago but which now need to be ended in mutual freedom. We come to understand better those roots in a larger love which both includes and transcends individual people. At more than one level 'we are one another', perhaps in an even wider way than when in remarkable seeming coincidences, Arthur Guirdham constantly found himself meeting people closely linked with him in past shared lives as Cathars. Entwined in many such memories there remains also, and no doubt will continue to remain, the wide problem of egotism which so often shuts out insight and all the values which are larger than itself.

9

It is impertinent to speak of the real self of the mentor. One is well out of one's spiritual depth if one attempts to measure his stature. Obviously it must far exceed one's own. The teacher can only teach because his soul knows more than the pupil. The pupil, if he is honest with himself, soon comes to know that it is never possible for him to 'see all round' his teacher. It is very much the other way round.

If the pupil listens carefully, then in time he recognises that occasionally concepts deeper than the mentor's normal ones are flashed swiftly into his consciousness. Without drawing attention, he offers this glimpse, and the pupil needs to learn to be awake to it if he can. The mentor's intention is to deepen the pupil's intuition. Sometimes he invites the pupil to come with him on a 'journey' into the inner world. Really this means a journey not in space but in consciousness: in order to follow, the pupil finds he must drop some of his present landmarks of thinking and feeling. The journey requires a

THE MENTOR

certain nakedness of spirit. This is hard to achieve and harder still to sustain at other times. In another lesson the pupil is sometimes said to have been shown a blueprint for his life programme. This is a hint to make a spring cleaning of his conscience, and to look for impulses long since lost, and now needing to be found again. He begins to bring back suggestions, maybe at first somewhat vague, for his spiritual attention to work upon. He becomes aware he needs to attune himself more carefully and more humbly. These are simple ways in which spiritual growth is slowly brought about.

An essential part of the adventure of working with a mentor is to recognise that the mentor is a way-shower and the way is often to discard.

So there will be both a personal and an impersonal pointing of the way.

Grace Cooke, the medium for the mentor White Eagle, was well aware of a deeper White Eagle who lay behind the wise, gentle, humorous White Eagle his pupils knew so well. This deeper White Eagle, though equally loving was more stern. 'We do not flatter' he once said, 'our love for you is pure'. The plural should be noted here. True mentors speak less as individuals than as a mouthpiece for a group. Grace Cooke was also aware that behind this deeper White Eagle there stood a greater mentor still. It is one of the marks of mentors that they too, as they tell us, take their instructions from those beyond them, and call upon their pupils to recognise the existence of this hierarchy of beings. No mentor stands alone, or speaks only for himself. The implications here are extremely important. It is a demonstration of the widening of vision, with many steps still awaiting on the long climb up the Jacob's Ladder of consciousness.

After death some mediums, and most pupils, recognise their mentor is a larger being than had been expected, 'How blessed we are' is a typical comment of a pupil. One medium said after his death, that in place of the former mentor he thought he knew so well, he now finds himself in awe of him and uncomfortable in his presence. His access to him too is now limited and mostly confined to attending his classes of instruction. He still has far to go to know him as he really is. Whatever the mystery, his stature clearly lies beyond this pupil's reach.

It follows too that if in reality they are large beings, the design with which they come will be large too. We are little acorns who will one day be a great tree, but, more important, a fragment of a great forest. The pattern, unfinished and undisclosed, upon which mentors expect to be working probably over the next several hundred years, can only gradually be glimpsed by a mentor's present pupil. Perhaps since the strongest pupils can know so little, it is wise to regard a mentor's work as an experiment in consciousness, of which, as a mentor has said, neither he nor we can yet see the outcome. It is a long-term process.

After a period of working with a true mentor it gradually becomes apparent that he bears within him a presence of holiness. As men find themselves letting go of their personal aims and efforts, now seen as puny indeed, they begin to tune towards this holiness, poured out upon the human scene from deeper sources than the mentor's own and available to all. Man's true future, it becomes clear, lies far beyond his present understanding. It is the long-term self the mentor is interested in. If you break your leg or lose your fortune, he doesn't really mind much; he stands apart from the concern, the pleasure-pain syndrome which is yours rather than his. It then becomes clear he sees his charge as something more extensive than how the little earth personality fares. He wants to free his friend to be his larger being; he wants to make the genie emerge from the bottle, the chick peck its way out of the confining shell. Does it not resemble the process spoken of in the parables of the Kingdom of Heaven? The teacher, like many others within other disciplines, is supplying the leaven.

THE MENTOR

To illustrate the sort of theme these teachers talk about, let us look at a controversial aspect, already touched upon: the causality of the inner world – as far as we can understand it – does require this concept of reincarnation. We have already asked what has happened to all these other selves we must have lived. Do we, whilst on earth, have a degree of access to them in some inner part of ourselves? A mentor who, to me, is of senior stature puts it like this:

> . . . you have already developed a number of other personalities in past incarnations. The sum total of all these . . . incarnations goes to the building of the permanent self . . . the temple which is being built in the heavens . . . the higher self . . . After death . . . the lower elements of personality, that part which . . . is no longer useful . . . fall(s) away and disintegrate(s) . . . the part which has been built into that personality of a more durable nature, continues to live, and is absorbed in due course into the higher self, or temple of the soul . . . These personalities can be reassumed at any time, they are not lost.

As has been said, it is likely that a mentor borrows one of these old personalities from the wardrobe of his being, but he is certainly much more than this person. He animates it for the time being, because only so can he approach our present levels at all. In other words, on his pathway into the interior worlds, he has abandoned any attachment to his earth personalities, making himself free of them.

The purpose of communicators of stature is thus twofold. The first is to lead one on to achieve the immediate task of the present incarnation – almost invariably partly bound up with personality limitations to be overcome.

Their second task is to help one to express whilst on earth a little more of one's true identity, and of what is open to that identity. More parts of it are drawn gradually into daily consciousness and thus enrich life. In spiritual things, one is always confronting paradox: at times in order to assimilate one has to throw logic away. Thus one is offered simultaneously a limitation and an expansion; on the one hand a painful and humdrum task, and on the other, right of access to a treasure. The limitation is the bread of life; the expansion is the wine. The aspects we are sent, or send ourselves, back to earth to cultivate can well need intensive care, a care which involves a limitation of being in order to cultivate the missing but necessary quality. If a man was a bad-tempered musician last time, then next time he may have the temper but not the music. It is his little packet of karma.

It is best to sup on both bread and wine. It is likely that his life will offer a special opportunity to cure the former bad temper. It very likely also offers the chance to grow new qualities required to come to flower perhaps in a later incarnation more fully than now. Here is encountered a beautiful law of spiritual economy. We are permitted to reach, if we can, any part of our whole being we are able to find and utilise for its beauty and for the profit of others in our present life, with the exception of such part of it, which if re-exercised might beguile us away from the specific redemptive task for which a present limitation is needed. Hence the bad-tempered musician next time might find himself lacking a musical ear; that is then a limiting fence which, for his own good, he cannot climb over.

Much of the path is made up of regeneration in its negative sense but also in its positive mode of re-generation, that of being born again. He brings about this change or metanoia, recognising a new man within him. In this process, often unrewarding to the former man, the mentor is waiting and watching, not least when to the pupil he seems entirely absent. Such phases have to be part of his ministering. In other modes he is present as the one with the lighted lamp, the way-shower, or as leader of a group in which the pupil may not at all fully be sure either of his fellow companions in the group nor of his own particular role. In this enterprise of finding the inner self, darkness is as productive as light. The pupil hopes and learns to utilise both.

This freedom, brought about through the shedding of the personality, takes long to recognise. The wearing of the mask and disguise of a tiresome (because unresolved) earth personality will not be ended, but each time the inner man, by the help of this imperfect mask which is yet part of himself, will become gradually transformed. Thus does the frog in the legend turn gradually into the prince. If it is true that in essence we already belong to this inner world, how is it that so many are quite unaware of it? The answer could hardly be simpler – because our attention is elsewhere, our eyes are turned towards earth matters which engross us, or to which our own nature forces us to attend. Wounded as we are, we are voluntarily or involuntarily facing our 'unfinished business' from earlier lives. The inner world is waiting and open, but it can be perfectly right for us to fulfil also tasks geared to the everyday world. To perform such tasks is a proper aim provided it is judged by its motives. Let it not be said though that true motives are always easy to discover. One's most skilful lies are those one tells to oneself.

In moral terms, the right outer task is as good as the right inner one. It is simply that they make demands on different parts of our nature. Few things are more indecorous or blunting than to take upon oneself a moral superiority for the choice we make.

There is an aspect of instruction also from the opposite pole of oneself, the earth laggard who somewhere knows he is on a journey as does the more shapely inner self. In the mystery of experience each is beholden to the other, and gives and demands patience. The question so often asked, in the séance room and in many other places, 'Why has this happened to me?' receives an answer from the part of the self which does not ask the question. The inner self will acquiesce in the experience even when the question-asking personality turns away from his answer in rage or disgust. By one route or another the inner self is always available waiting and ready to respond.

Recognition comes by raising the consciousness away from long-held things, and by learning to look anew at a more patient level. When this happens, the man within begins to say 'Of course, I had forgotten'. So, somewhere, he has known all the time. To be a rational being, however useful, is to miss some of the more subtle chains of causation within, which elude the reason, in a somewhat similar way to how the hidden statements of art conceal themselves from reason, but once seen are immediately taken to heart. The critic limps behind the artist.

In the world of spiritual teaching one trains to unravel part at least of what life is putting before one; to learn not to adapt the teaching to oneself but to adapt oneself to the teaching, and to know, where one refuses, if the refusal is foolish. One seeks and finds the place of inner silence and there one truly comes to know.

The mentor, with his mastery of truths at a number of levels of consciousness is without doubt the key figure in the field of communication. To find him securely needs an unwavering discipline. To find, recognise and then put to heartfelt use, is the task through which the pupil receives, acts, and then gives his thanks.